Asian Values and Human Rights

Asian Values and Human Rights

A CONFUCIAN COMMUNITARIAN
PERSPECTIVE

Wm. Theodore de Bary

HARVARD UNIVERSITY PRESS
Cambridge, Massachusetts
London, England
1998

Library of Congress Cataloging-in-Publication Data
De Bary, William Theodore, 1919–
Asian values and human rights : a Confucian communitarian
perspective / Wm. Theodore de Bary.
p.   cm.
Includes bibliographical references and index.
ISBN 0-674-04955-1 (alk. paper)
1. Human rights—Asia.   2. Social values—Asia.
3. Confucianism—Asia.   4. Communitarianism—Asia.
I. Title.
JC599.A78D4—1998
323'.095—dc21   97-46726

To Brett, Paul, Cathy, and Bea

Acknowledgments

This book is based in part on lectures given at the University of Hawaii and East-West Center in January 1997 to inaugurate the Wing-tsit Chan Memorial Lectureship, which is to be held in alternate years at Columbia University and the University of Hawaii with a grant from the Chiang Ching-Kuo Foundation. I wish to thank Professor Roger Ames, head of the University's Center for Chinese Studies, and Larry Smith, Dean of Education at the East-West Center, for their help in initiating these lectures. Other portions of the book draw upon work done for other occasions, especially the conferences on Confucianism and Human Rights held at the East-West Center under the auspices of Dean Smith.

Also distilled herein is work I have done for, and discussions I have had with members of the Neo-Confucian Seminar at Columbia; and with colleagues at meetings of the International Confucian Association in Beijing, Qufu and the Yue-lu Academy, Changsha, China; at symposia held in Paris by the Joint Committee for Cooperation on East Asian Studies, under the leadership of Professor Leon Vandermeersch of the École Francaise d'Extrême Orient, Paris, and Professors Jacques Gernet and Pierre-Etienne Will of the Collège de France; and at Castel Gandolfo, Italy, under the auspices of Pope John Paul II and the Institute of Human Sciences, Vienna.

In the preparation of the book for publication I also wish to acknowledge helpful suggestions from Jeff Kehoe of Harvard University Press, as well as the assistance of Martin Amster, Marianna Stiles, and, as always, Fanny Brett de Bary.

Contents

Asian Values and Human Rights

1

"Asian Values" and Confucianism

When I was first asked by the National Endowment for Democracy to speak on "Asian values" at a conference entitled "The Future of Democracy in Asia," the sponsors themselves admitted that they had only a vague notion of what Asian values were all about, and hoped I might give them a clue. Unfortunately, fifty years of studying, teaching, and writing about Asian civilizations and Asian humanities did not help much in answering the question. "Asian values" is a new concept in current political parlance, and one could not help wondering what this new usage was all about.

From the recent debates on multiculturalism one might suspect a reference here to the Asian component of the term Asian-American, which has come to represent the infusion into American life of cultural values from one or another group of Asian extraction, now claiming recognition as minorities in a new multicultural America. Values ordinarily connote the core or axial elements of a culture, the traditional ground (mostly seen as moral but not exclusively so) on which rest the culture's most characteristic and enduring institutions. Asian American, however, refers to a set of several ancestral cultures, each the product of a particular homeland in Asia whence came the immigrant group, and each proud of its own distinctive traditions. Paradoxically then, the minorities included under the rubric Asian-American find their only unity (if it is not to be found in the common experience of victimization) in the joint claim to diversity. Nothing there of common ancestry or core Asian values.

True, there is a special sense in which scholars from different parts of Asia, on coming to America, have contributed to the translation and interpretation of their own culture in Western terms, while at the same time doing so from a new Asia-wide perspective, which sometimes has lead to the recognition of shared values among Asians. This scholarly recognition itself, however, is part of a larger world trend, the undoubted importance of which is limited neither to Asia nor America, nor to any ethnic or scholarly group.

In historical fact, while the diverse cultures of Asia are each to some degree multicultural (that is, the products of long cultural interactions), there was, until modern times, no consciousness among them of a shared Asian identity. Even as a defensive reaction to pressures from the West in the nineteenth and twentieth centuries, Pan-Asianism has mostly been adjunct to modern nationalism and instrumentally subservient to it, rather than constituting anything like an Asian people's cultural bedrock. Traditionally the distinct civilizations of Asia did not identify themselves with a common continental culture, whatever the religious bonds they may have shared with other Asian peoples. Even Samuel Huntington, that adept descryer of clashing civilizations on the contemporary power scene, has found no common "Asian Culture" or "Asian Civilization," but only—up to this point, at least—irreducible differences among the major Asian civilizations.

Such being the case, one naturally suspects that the expression Asian values, a relatively recent construct, is meant to suit other ideological purposes, as was the case in pre–World War II Japan, with its proclamation of a "Greater East Asian Co-Prosperity Sphere," imagining that other Asian peoples would identify with this Japanese formulation of a hybrid Asian ideology resistant to Western domination.

Today the most likely source for such a concept is Singapore, a city-state with a Eurasian culture and ethnically mixed Asian (but predominantly Chinese) population. Singapore has a genuine need to formulate some value consensus among diverse—and potentially divisive—ethnic and religious groups that will serve as a common denominator for public morality, for the civil conduct of public affairs, and for the work ethic that is needed to sustain a high level of economic growth.

This understandable need and concern in Singapore is conditioned by other limiting factors, however. Prime among these is a belief in ruling circles that only strong, steady leadership can keep communal peace, and that authoritarian government, providing firm policy direction and social stability, is the necessary condition of continued economic growth. It is here, then, that the Singaporean conception of Asian values has become identified with authoritarian rule and the two together brought into collision with modern human rights concepts and practices.

That Singapore should be taken as a model for Hong Kong is hardly surprising, given the similarities in their geographic situations and their shared Sino-British political and cultural backgrounds. But that the tiny city-state of Singapore, hardly an imperial power, should now be seen as the fountainhead of inter-continental resistance to the human rights movement is suggested by a report from Africa. This *New York Times* report suggests that authoritarian regimes on that continent, seeking to emulate the economic success of Singapore and other East Asian nations, have adopted what is called an Asian model of development,[1] giving priority to the strengthening of state authority, central control, and social discipline, rather than to the development of democratic institutions.

What is most striking in this report is its further identification of the Asian model of development with Confucianism, an idea that could only have come from Singapore itself. Before the latter's rise to economic and political prominence, Confucianism had often been considered a drag on economic development and modernization. While this early stigmatizing of Confucianism as backward and retrograde had begun to yield, in the sixties and seventies, to a revisionist view of East Asia's (especially the so-called Little Dragons') "post-Confucian" culture as a powerful human resource for modernization, it was Singapore's Lee Guan-yew who most visibly dramatized the combination of authoritarian direction, high-speed economic progress, and the promotion of Confucian values. (Taiwan could well have qualified for the same role, since its economic, technological, and social successes were no less impressive than Singapore's and its continuity of Confucian culture was even better attested, but in these same years, Taiwan, rather than pitting Confucian values against democracy and human rights, was moving in the other direction—away from one-party tutelage by the Kuomintang and towards a more representative electoral democracy.)

Thus, if "Asian values" remains a problematic concept in this context, the expression "non-Western," prejudicial though its negative connotations may be for other cultures, could actually apply here. When authoritarian regimes in far-off Africa declare themselves cousin to similar states in Asia, it cannot be that they spring from the same ethnic or cultural roots but that a common cause is defined negatively in resistance to certain Western democratic values that they see as needlessly complicating the task of economic development.

Neither genuinely Asian, nor necessarily the development model for all of Asia (considering the success of Japan, South Korea, and Taiwan in combining economic growth with progress towards liberal democracy), this authoritarian model is dressed up in supposed "Confucian values," a notion that may have a certain specious plausibility considering the widespread tendency, earlier in this century, to identify Confucianism with autocratic and authoritarian rule in the imperial dynasties—a view widely propagated in both China and the West after the collapse of the Manchu dynasty in 1911.

What has lent further credence to this association of Confucianism with authoritarianism is the more recent reversal of Communist China's long-standing hostility to Confucianism—typified earlier by the Cultural Revolution's targeting of it as the ghost of the past hampering revolutionary change. Since the death of Mao, however, and the overthrow of the so-called Gang of Four, Confucianism has been discreetly rehabilitated by the more moderate Deng and Jiang regimes—with considerable assistance from Singapore—as a better long-term support for an established government than the revolutionary, class-struggle morality that had inspired its rise to power, but later had torn the country apart in the days of Mao.

At the height of the Cultural Revolution, when Confucianism was under the most violent attack, this repudiation of Chinese culture seemed to me not the last word in this debate. As I said in the early 1970s:

> The Chinese have thought of the Way (or Dao) as a growing process and expanding force. At the same time, following Mencius, they have felt that this Way could not be real or genuine for them unless somehow they could find it within themselves, as something not external or foreign to their own nature.[2] The unfortunate aspect of their modern experience has been the frustrating of that healthy instinct, through a temporary loss of their own self-respect and a denial of their right to assimilate new experience by a process of reintegration with the old. To have seen all value as coming solely from the West or as extending only into the future, and not also as growing out of their own past, has hindered them in recent years from finding that Way or Dao within themselves. The consequences of that alienation and its violent backlash have been only too evident in the Cultural Revolution. We may be sure, however, that the process of growth is only hidden, not stopped, and that the new experience of the Chinese people will eventually be seen in significant part as a growth emerging from within and not simply as a revolution inspired from without.[3]

Nevertheless, it is understandable that the present regime, following the more moderate policies of Deng Xiaoping, feels some nervousness about too abrupt a reversal in its legitimizing ideology. Its totalitarian party structure and its claim to one-party rule—to the monopolization of politics that it still guards jealously—are based on the idea of the Communist Party's unprecedented historic success in reunifying the country militarily, establishing firm control, and revolutionizing it economically. Lest it needlessly jeopardize this precarious claim to legitimacy, the current leadership is still somewhat reserved in its sponsorship of the Confucian revival and careful to channel it in directions considered conducive to harmony, stability, and continuity.

Meanwhile, critics of the Deng regime, many of them still motivated by the libertarian ideals of the May Fourth Movement out of which the Chinese Communist Party itself was born in 1921, and by the militant anti-establishmentarianism of the Cultural Revolution in the late sixties and early seventies, are only confirmed in their negative view of Confucianism when they see it adopted by the current, repressive regime. All the more are they persuaded of this when they see advocates of a distinctively Chinese form of socialism cite Confucianism as the essence of the Chinese tradition, and invoke it as the native cultural ground on which to reject human rights concepts as alien, culture-bound, Western impositions on China. The modern "liberationist" movement (and its heirs at Tiananmen) who had, as an article of faith, taken the emancipation of the individual to be a prime goal of the revolution, were dismayed but probably by this time not surprised to find the Deng regime suppressing human rights as being incompatible with the traditional Confucian values of harmony and social discipline. This fit the picture of a reactionary Confucianism they had been given earlier.

It was not, however, the Confucianism of Chinese scholars carrying on Confucian studies abroad, free from the depredations of the Cultural Revolution, nor was it the view of human rights held by others conversant with both Confucian tradition and Western human rights thinking for whom the two were not incompatible. When the Universal Declaration of Human Rights was adopted by the United Nations in 1948, participants in the process included representatives from the Republic of China, schooled in Western law but also disposed to include Confucian humanistic sentiments in the language of that Declaration.[4]

Ironically one of these representatives was Wu Teh-yao, later president of Tung-hai University in Taiwan, who still later became the director of the Institute of East Asian Philosophies, which promoted the Confucian revival in Singapore in the eighties. Men of this generation, liberally educated in both China and the West, included Dr. Hu Shih, a one-time president of Beijing University and subsequently head of the Academia Sinica in Taiwan; the jurist Dr. John C. H. Wu; Dr. T. F. Tsiang, China's permanent representative at the United Nations, and many others who saw Western and Confucian values as convergent in these respects, not necessarily at odds. Indeed Hu Shih, out of the Chinese experience, added to the list of human rights. Witnessing how his countrymen in the People's Republic were forced to speak against their own consciences, he proposed adding, to the right of freedom of speech, the freedom not to speak.

This earlier Chinese judgment has been confirmed by at least two subsequent developments. Japan, Taiwan, and South Korea—all countries whose civil cultures have been deeply influenced by Confucianism—have subscribed to the Universal Declaration of Human Rights and generally have observed its provisions (in the cases of Taiwan and South Korea, with the record of observance improving as democratic institutions have evolved). For the People's Republic, however, the record is mixed. On the one hand the government has formally subscribed to the Universal Declaration, and its constitution has made legal provision for human rights. This was without any stated reservations as to how compatible these might be with Confucian values—a tacit admission, it would seem, of the difficulty of constructing a Confucian or Chinese rationale for opposing them. On the other hand, as is well known, the People's Republic of China has frequently been charged by international bodies with violations of human rights in China and Tibet. Officially the response to such charges has been simply to reject them as interference in the internal affairs of China. It is then left to others, less formally but with implicit official approval, to argue the case that the West's conception of human rights is too individualistic, and out of keeping with China's communitarian traditions based on Confucianism.

At this point the rhetoric of nationalism and of China's resistance to Western imperialism comes powerfully into play, now in the form of allegations that Western culture-bound concepts of human rights are being imposed on China. To deflect and discredit charges that individual human rights are being violated in China, sweeping counter-accusations are made that "rampant individualism" in the United States and the West has produced a pattern of gross self-indulgence and social decay that Asian nations cannot afford and must guard against by tough law enforcement.

Although spokesmen for authoritarian regimes like to define the human rights problem as one of the "individualistic West" versus "communitarian Asia," this formulation only obscures the issue. The very real social problems attributed to the "individualistic West"—violence, crime, drug and sex abuse, and breakdown of family life, to name only the most obvious—attend the modernization process wherever it goes on, in East or West. Thus it is less a question of Asian versus Western values than a problem of how the forces of a runaway economic and technological modernization are eroding traditional values in both Asia and the West. Since these erosive effects are felt particularly by the individual and the community in the form of damage to one's sense of personhood, a decline in individual self-respect, and a loss of the sense of belonging to any stable, viable community, it is natural for these trends to become matters of deep anxiety and concern. The solution of these problems is only prejudiced, however, when they are misconceived as conflicts between East and West, or in ways that further belittle the individual and degrade the community, which is what happens when human rights issues are treated primarily as questions of law and order and the upholding of state authority.

As the rhetorical heat rises, in the crossfire of charges and countercharges no middle ground is left for a rational resolution of human rights issues. Still, much as one would like to escape this confrontational mode and lower the temperature of the debate, it is questionable whether one should try to allay mutual defensiveness or escape a recriminatory atmosphere at the cost of ignoring real issues. The Clinton administration, having first blown hot on human rights, has now blown cold, and is even worse off for having beaten an ignominious retreat. Political realism may dictate this, since governments can go only so far in pressuring others without exposing themselves to charges of interference in others' domestic affairs. Yet there is a more subtle reason that sets a limit to what can be accomplished through government channels, a factor no less real for being intangible: diplomacy, by its very nature, requires tact; it cannot succeed if the other party is discountenanced and left humiliated. In this case one may well ask whether it was not Clinton, rather than the Chinese, who lost face, but in the wake of this recent human rights fiasco, one wonders whether other approaches are not needed, especially non-governmental ones, to matters of such delicacy. Non-governmental organizations can speak clearly for themselves in ways that diplomats cannot. Scholars, journalists, editorialists, and publicists can, in settings less fraught with tension, argue more intently and probe more deeply into the underlying issues.

Through dialogue, and even open debate where that becomes possible, questions of Confucianism and human rights can be clarified better than they have been so far, so as to move beyond the level of the shouting match. In the process one could hope to recognize both shared human values, significant cultural differences, and limiting economic factors that condition the effective realization of certain humane values.

At this point, however, I should note a distinction long made by serious students of Confucianism (as of other traditions as well) between ideal values and their implementation in historical practice. Both must be taken into account in any fair assessment of a tradition's relevance to modern life, as when it is claimed by proponents of "Asian values" that Confucianism has a special pertinence to the modernization process and to the practical formulation of human rights concepts in Asia. Because of the special Confucian concern for the defining of human moral relations in particular social contexts, we need to think of traditional values as transmitted on different social levels and in diverse institutional forms, rather than as constituents of an unvarying, monolithic system. Current political controversy and ideological polemics rarely take such distinctions and particularities into account, but they are essential to meaningful discourse and are not to be dismissed as just fussy academic distinctions.

In the response to "Asian values" claims it has sometimes been thought sufficient to find in Asian traditions, and mostly in classical Confucian writings, some evidence of values akin to those associated with human rights concepts. For this purpose quotations have been drawn from the *Analects* of Confucius, or in the case of Buddhism from the sutras or the pronouncements of the early Indian ruler Asoka, to illustrate their humanitarian sentiments.[5] This book too will necessarily refer to the body of classical Confucian literature in order to establish the original premises of the tradition more precisely than has usually been the case when Confucian values were invoked. Still, such classic statements serve only a limited purpose. They can illustrate traditional ideals or axial values—which are by no means insignificant—but they do not, in themselves, speak to the historical realities of China in later times or to the twentieth-century circumstances in which contemporary human rights issues are embedded.

What happened in the course of history to the Confucians' attempts to implement and live by ancient ideals is of crucial importance. How things worked out in practice, and if it is possible to identify them, what were the limiting conditions in which Confucians tried to act upon and work out these ideals are questions quite relevant both to the implementation of human rights and the pursuit of economic development today. Problems of continuity and change in the evolution of major traditions must be considered. Confucianism should not be thought either static or monolithic—that is, taking the sayings of Confucius and Mencius just by themselves, to represent an historically developing, often conflicted, and yet gradually maturing Confucian tradition. Nor should it be seen as simply adapting itself to just any historical situation, so that the heirs of Mao Zedong could claim it as their own even after Mao had done his best to disown it. Mao's Great Proletarian Cultural Revolution may have had its distinctive Chinese characteristics, but the complicity of the Chinese Communist Party in the violent anti-Confucian campaigns of the 1960s and 1970s hardly qualifies it today for the role of custodian and expounder of Confucian tradition.

In the matter of communitarianism there is also the question of whether Asia and China can be conceded exclusive rights to speak for it, and whether Western conceptions of human rights can be dismissed as bespeaking only a radical individualism or self-indulgent permissiveness (the "spiritual pollution" that is said to contaminate Western liberalism and endanger the Asian community). The forms of Western communitarianism are themselves legion and of long-standing; even the contemporary versions range widely over the political spectrum, reflecting the evolution of nineteenth-century Western liberalism into twentieth-century socialist or social democratic varieties (with liberals often characterized as "pinko") and spoken for more recently by writers as diverse as Christopher Lasch, Amitai Etzioni, Michael Sandel, Charles Taylor, and Alasdair MacIntyre, some of whom may even be labeled neo-conservatives.

Though it might be of some use to compare the communitarianisms of these Western writers, and especially what they have to say about human rights, with what is said about these rights by the Asian values school (who in any case are rarely specific in their objections), it is not to be expected that the former would endorse the latter's derogation of human rights, and far more likely that they would support the Universal Declaration. Hence I shall undertake no such inventory or assessment of their views here. Rather the special focus of this book will be to consider what communitarianism has meant in the Confucian context, that is, in the longer development of Confucianism and especially of Neo-Confucianism, as it attempted to deal with the problems of an increasingly complex society, dominated by an authoritarian state.

The latter story is a largely untold one, since Confucianism, seen as deeply implicated in the collapse of the old dynastic regime, has been in general disfavor for much of the twentieth century. Discounted in advance as essentially conservative and obsolescent, the Confucian experience, as shown in the voluminous record of Confucian statecraft concerns and practical efforts, has gone largely unnoticed until recently—unknown even to those who now claim to speak for "Confucian communitarianism," yet whose actual acquaintance with it, under Mao's rule, was limited to the clichés of an outworn revolutionary doctrine or to historical misreadings traceable to European-derived ideological misconceptions about Chinese history and society.

Chapters 4 and 5 of this book will deal with Confucian communitarian thought in relation to two specific cases: community schools *(she-xue)* and the community organizations known as "community compacts" *(xiang yue),* the fate of which is illustrative of a wider range of efforts by Confucians to strengthen community life and build consensual fiduciary institutions. If these two cases seem to be rather homespun and humdrum examples of communitarianism, they are nevertheless authentically Confucian, genuine expressions of a tradition that assigned a prime value to education and ritual—a value that endured well into the twentieth century. More than simply illustrative of the enduring importance of education to the Confucians, however, community schools, as a response to the specific historical opportunities and challenges in late Imperial China, are also indicative of the difficulties Confucians experienced in trying to put their educational ideals into practice.

The community compacts too are instructive of the same historical process and predicament. Like the schools themselves, they were thought of by Confucians as civilizing instruments, especially in the sense that these organs of consensual and cooperative self-governance were conceived as local rituals and not as instruments of state power, voluntaristic in nature and not coercive. Hence this authentically Confucian conception of civility as achieved by voluntary rites, locally observed, rather than by legal systems enforced by an overarching (and often over-reaching) state stands in ironic contrast to the current "Asian values" rendering of communitarianism as something readily and directly translatable into a law-and-order society dominated by an authoritarian central government.

The fact that both the community schools and community compacts fell victim to the hegemony of the dynastic state (as described in chapters 4 and 5) should not be taken as demonstrating their historical insignificance. On the contrary the noble failure of these Confucian experiments only underscores the very real difficulties of implementing ideal values, for all the classical, scriptural sanction behind them, in such a tough environment and such limiting conditions. One cannot assume that, in China today, it will be much easier for liberal democratic politics to become established in the face of similarly adverse circumstances; hence realism cautions against overly optimistic expectations. At the same time, if the difficulties are recognized, there may be less of a tendency to assume that progress is inevitable—that economic liberalization will necessarily lead to political liberalization, or that Confucian humanistic influences can be counted on as a long-term force for good, without the need for active advocacy.

Together these two earlier communitarian efforts, had they been successful, might have contributed to a Confucian version of a civil society. The mere existence of relatively independent local organizations, however, would not alone have assured such an outcome. Such local entities did indeed exist in the form of traditional family, clan, and lineage organizations and religious communities that were largely autonomous. But the enjoyment of such autonomy is not the same thing as participation in a civil society, wherein organizations intermediate between family and state would serve as a political infrastructure, with formal channels of communication leading upward to policy-making levels on top and at the center. Had organizations come into being that would have expanded education, extended literacy more widely, and provided public channels (open media) for the more active participation of the people in representative government, something of a civil society (no doubt still with Confucian and Chinese characteristics) might have emerged.

That such did not happen points to the other side of the state-society equation: the absence of a constitutional order providing formally for the kind of countervailing institutions identified in the West with civil society. This is not simply a matter of delimiting the power of the state, for in practice there had always been limits to effective state control, and many local organizations enjoyed virtual autonomy. Besides the limiting of imperial rule itself, greater access to power and decision making at the top—that is greater participation in the political process—would have had to be provided by a constitutional structure. And indeed the two would have had to go hand in hand, for without popular support, educated and informed opinion, and a moral culture supportive of it, any constitution itself would have been a dead letter.

It is the contention of chapter 6 that some of the best Confucian minds were themselves coming to such a realization in the pre-modern period, and that therefore a constitutional order supportive of some liberal democratic values and human rights, though not at all an assured prospect on Confucian grounds or Chinese calculations alone, nevertheless was not an idea totally foreign to Confucian thinking nor out of line with the growing critique of dynastic rule. Evidence for this view comes from the subsequent acknowledgment of the need for such constitutional processes by Confucian spokesmen in the twentieth century and from the ready adoption of them by other East Asian societies sharing in Confucian cultural influences.

In relation to the Confucian preference for rites over laws, however, the need for a constitutional order to replace dynastic law points to a weakness in the Confucian approach to government insofar as it relied so heavily, and unavailingly, on the moral restraints of ritual to curb the excesses of autocratic power.

The same question arises when one considers the status of women as an area of particular concern for human rights. Here too, as detailed in chapter 7, we find that Confucian concerns for human dignity and norms of ritual respect for the human person were insufficiently borne out in the actual status and treatment of women, and, in fact, were contradicted by some of the severe limitations imposed on women in the name of Confucian ritual. Indeed this very tension within Confucianism and Chinese society may account for the comparative susceptibility, rather than determined resistance to, Western standards in this respect by Confucian-influenced societies in East Asia.

This is not, of course, the same thing as saying that an improvement in the condition of women would likely have occurred without the catalyst of outside influence—an outcome that is frankly implausible. Even so, in this area as in the others to be considered later, there is little evidence to suggest that an Asian defense against human rights could be mounted on fundamental Confucian grounds, and good reason to believe that the Confucian historical experience would lend positive support to many of the human rights enumerated in the Universal Declaration, as well as negative confirmation of the need for others of them.

The nominal acceptance of such rights or even their legal enactment (as is now almost universal in East Asian constitutions) still leaves a large question as to whether effective compliance with them will follow. This is why the question of civil society, more than just a side issue, becomes rather a crucial one in the discussion of Asian communitarianism. It is one thing to dispute the claim that Confucianism supports a strong state and systems of authoritarian, law-and-order rule. It is another thing to assert, but essential to do so, that without the elements of a civil society—meaning a practical infrastructure and countervailing institutions able to check the monopolization and abuse of state power—mere lip-service to human rights would count for little. If the proponents of Asian values are genuinely concerned, as they profess to be, with achieving a proper balance between the rights of the individual and the legitimate needs and claims of society, then for them the Confucian experience can be seen as truly relevant to the keeping of such a balance, and the Chinese historical record in these matters worth reflecting upon in this connection.

In what follows, I should like to address (if only in brief, general terms) the status of the individual in relation to family and state; rights as understood in Chinese law and Confucian ritual; school and community as they affect the question of a "communitarian" conception of human rights; and constitutionalism and civil society in China, as well as the status of women and women's education, as they relate to the implementation of such rights.

2

Individualism and Personhood

From the standpoint of the Chinese population as a whole, the family was the predominant social and economic institution in an agricultural society, and in many respects it furnished the theoretical model for other institutions such as the patriarchal dynastic state. But as a literate tradition Confucianism was also concerned from the start with individuals in relation to each other, as well as with the role of the scholar-official in his relations with the ruler and other scholars, teachers, and students.

Classically the paradigm of human relationships was stated by Mencius as:

> Between parent and child there is to be affection
> Between ruler and minister, rightness
> Between husband and wife, [gender] distinctions
> Between older and younger [siblings] an order of
>   precedence
> Between friends, trustworthiness.
> [Mencius 3A:4]

Since this paradigm was strongly reaffirmed in later (especially Neo-Confucian) tradition, as well as in other East Asian countries, we should note some of its implications. First, it focuses on human moral relationships and the priorities among them, particularly within the family. The setting of personal priorities and making of value distinctions is fundamental to Confucianism.

Next it should be noted that all of these relations involve reciprocity. The obligations are differentiated but mutual and shared. Thus, for instance, the relation between parents and child is not characterized exclusively in terms of the filial duty of child to parent, but in terms of mutual affection; and in other formulations of the husband/wife relationship, the same mutual affection and love is stressed.

It is also true that the respect for precedence (seniority), here identified particularly with the sibling relationship, was more broadly generalized in practice to apply to all five relationships, so that, for instance, the relationship of friends, here spoken of in terms of *xin*, mutual trust and reliability and thus based on mutuality and equality, was often analogized to that of older and younger brother (i.e., fictively, between persons who were not actually blood relations). Similarly the relation of ruler and minister was in later discourse often analogized to that of parent and child (though this was also disputed by leading Confucians, who saw the ruler/minister relationship as a collegial one).

Nevertheless, in this classic formulation of moral relations it is as striking that the ruler/minister relationship should contain no reference to loyalty as it is noteworthy that the parent/child relationship should lack any reference to filial piety. In later common (popular) discourse loyalty and filial piety are often spoken of as the typical Confucian virtues, and it is to this customary Confucian formula that implicit reference is made by those today who look to Confucianism as a support for superior authority. Yet loyalty and filial piety are totally missing here. From this one can see the incongruity in the recent news from Singapore, reporting the enactment of legal processes to compel children to meet their filial obligation to support their parents. Chinese law, it is true, traditionally recognized the importance of filial obligation, and the state often honored it, but it was considered rare and abnormal for such cases to come before a magistrate. Such matters were to be settled in the home or local neighborhood. And it is clear that Confucius, as recorded in the *Analects*, would have nothing to do with mindless conformism or coercive measures to enforce filial duty. Many passages affirm Confucius's belief that a forced or mechanical conformity to the norms of filial duty was not filial piety at all.[1] Indeed, Confucius pointedly insisted on moral cultivation and consensual social rituals, rather than legal compulsion, as the way to deal with such human problems. This underscores how pertinent to the present situation is the historic experience of China with a genuine, but neglected tradition of Confucian ritual in the authentic communitarian, rather than the authoritarian, law-and-order form.

Those familiar with high Confucian tradition and its finer nuances would be more conscious of the particular implications of Mencius's dwelling on the ruler/minister relation rather than on what is sometimes translated as "ruler/subject." Insofar as any subject might participate in governance, the same principle would apply, but in fact, as Mencius well understood, most "subjects" did not so participate in the political process, and what Mencius had in mind (as is the case later on with most Confucian scholarly literature) was the particular but at the same time mutual obligation of ruler and minister to adhere to what is right, and to consider the relationship at an end if they cannot agree on what is right. In this case undying loyalty attaches to principle, not persons.

In modern times awareness of this basic Confucian teaching has often been lost, and superficial notions of unquestioning loyalty to the ruler have taken over. But as late as the Ming and Qing dynasties, Mencius was well understood by those familiar with his teachings as reaffirmed by the great Neo-Confucian scholar-teacher Zhu Xi. Spectacular cases can be cited of heroic Confucian ministers standing up for what was right against all the despotic power of Ming rulers. One of the most celebrated cases is that of the outstanding Confucian scholar/minister Fang Xiaoru (1357–1402). Fang defied the Yongluo Emperor, who tried to silence him by threatening death not only to Fang himself but to all his kin as far as the ninth degree of relationship, if Fang did not cease his remonstrance against the Emperor. Fang did not yield, and all his family paid the price.

Another case is that of the Ming official Hai Rui (1513–1587), whose martyrdom was cited in the Mao era by the historian and playwright Wu Han as an example of courageous criticism of the ruler. In this instance Hai Rui's example was taken as an oblique reference to Peng Dehuai, a critic of Mao Zedong's policies. Mao, while encouraging people to speak out, reserved to himself the right to have them punished for it, as, indeed, Peng and Wu were.

An even more revealing example of the "freedom of speech" issue is the case of the founding emperor of the Ming, Taizu (r. 1368–1398), no less of a despot for being a peasant and populist. Taizu sought to reserve to himself the prerogative of offering the ritual sacrifice to Confucius, and to withdraw this privilege (with its accompanying authority) from local Confucian officials who had performed it since at least the Tang dynasty. Then, after expurgating the text of *Mencius* (used in the civil service examinations) of what he considered contumacious passages insulting to rulers, Taizu sought further to have Mencius's tablet removed from the Confucian temple. When his Confucian ministers objected, Taizu threatened death to any who opposed him, whereupon the minister Qian Tang, when he next came to court, brought with him a coffin, saying: "It would be an honor to die for Mencius."[2]

Taizu's attempt to suppress ministerial opposition goes to the heart of Mencius's dictum that the ruler/minister relationship should be governed by mutual respect for what is right. It is not, then, a matter of legal rights or of free speech in general, but of what Confucians would call proper respect or civility in the decorum that should prevail at court. In other words, it came under the Confucian heading of ritual decorum—of "rites" and not of legal rights or entitlements. (Indeed, in whatever ruling court or cabinet would not the conduct of such debate be a matter of personal decorum or civility, rather than one of legal rights?)

The further significance of the episode lies in the specificity of the personal relations involved. This is freedom of speech in the particular context of the ruler/minister relationship. By logical and natural extension it could apply to any subject who entered into such a personal or collegial association with the emperor (or into his official service), but ministerial remonstrance could not be taken as a right generally enjoyed by all subjects. It amounts then only to a restricted or limited freedom of speech, yet at the same time, asserted here as a basic human principle it is extendable to others who might assume that duty, and could become applicable to any wider extension of people's participation in the political process. In other words, embedded here in a particular personal, historical, and institutional context is a classic case of a Confucian universal human value. One could quibble about it and say that the Confucian case does not exactly fit the modern understanding of human rights, but if instead one is disposed to respect human values as experienced and expressed in different cultural settings, one could recognize here a rough parallel to the prophetic, protesting voice in other times and places, as in ancient Israel and thereafter in the Judeo-Christian tradition. Confucian "rightness" in the ruler/minister relation does not exactly correspond to the "righteousness" of God invoked by the Hebrew prophets, with which God's "people" were to identify themselves, but as it was associated in Confucianism with the order ordained by Heaven *(Tian)* this "rightness" had a universal aspect as well as a particularistic one: it characterized the special relationship of ruler and minister as meant to serve the larger public interest and general welfare *(gong)*.

On this basis, in the modern period reformers could take Confucian principle as indigenous Chinese cultural soil in which to ground legal rights and democratic institutions. Indeed, since the

Japanese in the late nineteenth and early twentieth century shared the same Confucian moral ground, they claimed it as the basis and rationale for the adoption of "people's rights" and parliamentary institutions in the Meiji period, to be followed in this shortly afterward by Chinese reformers who likewise sought to interpret Western democratic institutions in Confucian terms and transplant them to Chinese soil.

"Transplant" is a key word here, because it leaves open the question of how such institutions, developed in the West, could become rooted, grow, and thrive, or perhaps not, in soil that was admittedly foreign and yet at the same time recognizably human, irreducibly both common and diverse. To get a perspective on this modern adaptation, however, we must look further into the relationship of the individual and the community, so much at issue in the charge that Western human rights thinking is too individualistic for the more communitarian "Asian" traditions; then further we should consider this in relation to the Chinese historical process as it emerged from the time of Confucius and Mencius down through the imperial dynasties to the modern era. Indeed to my mind, the weakness of many discussions of China, Confucianism, and human rights, is that they tend to operate purely on the conceptual level—attempting to compare or contrast values in the abstract, rather than seeing how they have been observed and experienced in time, in a developing historical process.

First, let us examine the status of the "individual" in Confucian thought. Spokesmen for what is called an "Asian" communitarian position are not wrong in supposing that the concept of a radically free-standing, autonomous individual is foreign to Confucianism, but the contrast is more with the modern age than it is with some earlier Western traditions, themselves more communitarian, (or even with contemporary communitarian movements in the West that react against the recent trend). Modern libertarian individualism, as a product of rapid economic development and social change, presents the individual with a new abundance of "choices" to be made, while the extraordinary power of modern technology inspires and inflates the dream of unlimited expansiveness and liberation from all constraints. However, today these are phenomena of both East and West, wherever industrialization takes place; it is not a case of East *versus* West. Moreover, advocates of a traditional Asian "communitarianism" are wrong if they suppose—as Western writers too often have done—that in Confucianism the individual's worth is found only in the group, that he is no more than the sum of the social roles he is expected to perform, or that he is content with subordination to the group and established authority.

Confucius himself in the opening line of the *Analects* sets the matter in perspective when he speaks first of learning [from past tradition] and practicing it in the present; then of welcoming friends from afar [to share experiences with them]; and finally of characterizing the truly noble man as one who is unembittered even if he is unrecognized by others [especially the ruler]. The first two lines express the idea of a self shaped in the process of learning from others, but the last line conveys the sense that this should produce a person able to stand on his own. Later in the *Analects* this process is spoken of as "learning for one's self," in contrast to "learning for the sake of others' [approval],"—that is to say, for true self-development, rather than to gain social acceptance or political advancement.

This concept of a fully realized personhood is reaffirmed in Confucius' concise résumé of his own life experience:

> At fifteen I set my heart on learning.
> At thirty I was established [stood on my own feet].
> At forty I had no perplexities.
> At fifty I learned what Heaven commanded of me.
> By sixty my ear had become attuned to it.
> At seventy I could follow my heart's desire without transgressing.[3]

Here Confucius characterizes his life-long learning as centered on his own self-development and self-fulfillment in the course of meeting the demands of Heaven. If we are to judge from the rest of the *Analects,* what he learned had much to do with his relationship to others and his sense of responsibility for them, but here he describes his life experience as one of inner growth in response to the providential guidance of Heaven—Heaven as representing a higher moral authority in the universe, and Heaven's Way as defining his own mission in life. In his case "Heaven's command" *(Tianming)* is not the same as a dynastic mandate, though it shares with that mandate responsibility for what Heaven ordains morally and politically. Instead his is a very personal commission and vocation to public service that demands difficult and unexpected things of him, not easily accepted at first, but eventually bringing a sense of personal freedom and self-fulfillment.

This is no less true of the human condition and the human ideal as we see it in Mencius, for whom the Way and the imperatives of Heaven are found in the inmost depths of one's own being, just as the sense of "rightness *(yi)*" is said by him to spring from within one's deepest natural sentiments. Moreover, among the other two classic texts that for later Confucians constitute the canonical Four Books, the *Mean (Zhong yong),* while paying due respect to social roles and obligations, extols above all personal sincerity or integrity *(cheng),* which means being true to one's innermost self, especially when one is not observed by others or answerable to them. In the same vein the famous Eight Items of the *Great Learning* give clear priority in the first five items to the individual's self-development, before extending this further to family or state.

It is these texts and these concepts that later became formative of Neo-Confucian self-cultivation, reaffirming the morally responsible and affectively responsive self in the face of profound philosophical challenges from Buddhism and Daoism. And it is this same sense of the Way and its rightness, deep within one's self, from which a long line of Ming Neo-Confucian scholars from Qian Tang, Fang Xiaoru, Hai Rui and on down to Liu Zongzhou, drew the conviction and courage to challenge Ming despots. When one risks one's life in order to be true to one's own inmost self, it cannot be thought of as merely performing for others, fulfilling a social role or conforming to the values of the group. Though it would be equally inappropriate to call this self-centeredness simply a form of "individualism" (if by that one means individual freedom of choice or emancipation from social constraints), it does affirm a strong moral conscience, shaped and formed in a social, cultural process that culminates, at its best, in a sense of self-fulfillment within society and the natural order. Given its special Confucian features, one might call this a distinct "Confucian individualism," but I prefer the term "personalism" to "individualism," since it shares some common ground with forms of personalism in Western tradition as distinct from a modern liberationist "individualism." Here "personalism" expresses the worth and dignity of the person, not as a raw, "rugged" individual, but as a self shaped and formed in the context of a given cultural tradition, its own social community, and its natural environment to reach full personhood.[4]

On a portentous occasion in Hong Kong, anticipating its takeover by the People's Republic of China, Professor Anthony Yu of the University of Chicago discussed some of the issues at stake there. He described one factor threatening the future of education: the view that in China the collectivity always takes precedence over the individual, which inhibits the pursuit of truth for its own sake. Characterizing the Western educational tradition as "grounded upon the supreme good of individual self-fulfillment," he contrasted this to the Chinese tradition wherein "political and moral virtues unite as an indivisible homology in which the communal and collective take precedence over the individual."[5]

This is not a new view in the West, and of course, in China it is one the state is glad enough to accept. It remains nonetheless questionable as a characterization of the Confucian standpoint, which looked for a balanced relation between self and society. Although Confucius himself spoke for and to an educated class of scholar-officials, whose sense of political responsibility was inseparable from their privileged status as beneficiaries and custodians of a civilized learning tradition, he had little success himself in government and had to reconcile himself to a life of scholarship and teaching. In the end, however, he insisted that teaching and education themselves fulfilled the obligation of public service—one need not take office in order to fulfill this duty.[6]

No doubt Confucius had something of this in mind when he spoke, in the paradigmatic account of his own life-experience cited above, about how he came, albeit slowly and reluctantly, to accept what Heaven ordained for him: that is, learning in what capacity he could conscientiously fulfill Heaven's commission (his political vocation) as he tried to cope with the specific life situation Heaven presented to him—the difficulty he encountered in trying to obtain official employment on terms consistent with his principles. Could we perhaps call this belated discovery of his true vocation (teaching, not serving in office) an affirmation of "truth" as the supreme value? In Western terms, yes, we might, but in Confucian terms not exactly congruent with our own, it would more likely be expressed as Confucius's adherence to and following of the right Way *(Dao)*.

When taunted for his fastidious refusal to serve rulers if it meant being coopted by them for unworthy purposes, while yet he persisted stubbornly in the idealistic hope of political reform, Confucius replied: "One cannot herd with the beasts or flock with the birds. If I am not to serve in the company of other human beings (i.e., act as a responsible social being), then what am I to do? If the Way prevailed among men, I would not be trying to change things."[7]

Here Confucius insists on the following of the Way as a higher duty than simply taking office, and, without abandoning the moral struggle, persists in acting on behalf of the Way to reform an imperfect human society. Clearly he did not take service of the state, or subordination to the established order, as an ultimate obligation. Rather for him, pursuit of the Way came close to what Professor Yu has called "the pursuit of truth" in the West. Yet if one considers that both "Truth" in the West and the "Way" in China open out on unlimited horizons, and in some indefinable way ultimately converge, there would seem to be little use in drawing a fine line between them—much less in opening up a large chasm between East and West on this score.

The more relevant distinction to be made here is one Confucians drew between the Way of the Ruler and the Way of the Teacher. Ideally (in ancient legend) these two roles had been joined as one in the sage-kings, but by Confucius's time the Way had become split apart. For all later Confucians, Confucius as teacher and not as ruler was the personification of sageliness, the highest standard and model for anyone to follow. No later ruler ever commanded the same respect.

Another point of common confusion in regard to the issue of the individual versus the community or collectivity has been in positing the dichotomy of public *(gong)* and private *(si)* as necessarily an antithetical one—"public" as standing for the common good, and "private," negatively, for individual selfishness. It is true that these concepts are sometimes found in opposition, as when individual desires are seen to conflict with the common good. This is the case in the section on the "Evolution of Rites" in the *Record of Rites* compiled in the Han dynasty, which contrasts the primordial ideal of "all-under-Heaven as shared in common" *(Tianxia weigong)* with the historical reality of people pursuing their own private interests at others' expense—a social condition Confucius himself had to face and was unable to change, sage though he was. In the same *Record of Rites,* there is also a discussion of the opposition between "Heaven's principles" (identified here with the common good) and "human desires" (understood here to be "selfish"). In the given context however, this dichotomy refers to actions of the ruler that are selfish, when properly he should be acting in the common interest and holding himself to a higher, self-sacrificial standard of service to the public good.[8] Indeed, the implication of the passage is that the ruler should not indulge his own selfish desires at the expense of the people's legitimate desires, appetites, and material needs. It is not a question of ordinary persons sacrificing their natural desires to the group.

Thus, though "Heaven's principles" and "human desires" are juxtaposed in this case, it is not meant to suggest a necessary opposition or conflict between private and public, individual and collectivity, but rather to assert the obligation of rulers to uphold a public standard that keeps in balance individual desires and the common good. Even the great Confucian thinker, Xunzi, though he is generally identified with the view of human nature as evil, subscribed to this idea that the social order should aim at the satisfaction of people's desires.[9]

The same issue arises in the famous Han dynasty "Debate on Salt and Iron." Here the spokesmen for the state claim that their instituting of state monopolies over key resources, their maintaining of state marketing controls, and their general policy of state intervention in the economy is meant to defend the public interest against private exploitation. In this debate, however, spokesmen for the Confucians argue against this, charging that such regulation and intervention is contrary to the people's interest, which would be better served by a free market economy and private enterprise, allowing "the people" to act in their own interest and on their own initiative. In this debate, both sides claim to speak for the public interest, but it is the Confucians who argue that this interest is better served by encouraging the people's private initiative, while the bureaucrats' claim to speak for the public interest is questioned as only a cover for the pursuit of their own vested interests.

From this it may seem again that the Confucian ideal was a balance of public and private, not an assertion of one over the other. In fact, from the Confucian point of view the state's responsibility for the public interest was to encourage legitimate private initiative. How to define what was legitimate remained an issue, and the state, historically, was not slow to assert its own authority in this respect (any more than it is today), but Confucians were just as ready to challenge any such claim on the part of the state bureaucracy *(guan)*, asserting instead that the public interest *(gong)* consists in serving the legitimate desires and material needs of the people.[10] A balance of public and private *(gongsi yiti)*, not the person or individual subordinated to the collectivity or state, remained the Confucian ideal.

In much of what follows the historical dominance of the state will be apparent, but this being the fact, it is all the more important for us to recognize that its dominance did not go uncontested by the Confucians. Indeed, only in light of the continuing tension between the two can the true dimensions and complexity of the problem be appreciated.

3

Laws and Rites

In the Confucian world the self, from birth to death and into the after-life, was to be shown respect according to definite norms of behavior, spoken of as "rites" or "ritual decorum" *(li)* because of their association from earliest times with participation in family and clan religious rituals. Confucius saw this ritual decorum as an essential form of civility, fundamental to human governance and preferable to the attempted enforcement of laws. In the *Analects,* he says, "If you try to lead the people by regulations and order them by punishments, the people will evade these and have no sense of shame [in doing so]. If you lead them by virtue and order them through the rites, they will have a sense of shame and will correct themselves" [2:3].

This has usually been taken to express Confucius's strong distrust of law and his faith rather in the power of virtuous example. While not incorrect, this impression takes insufficient account of the importance Confucius attached to the second part of his formula: rites, as affirming and exemplifying norms of human conduct, including governance. For, given the high value placed on rites in the *Analects* generally, it is significant that Confucius here sees them as the most fundamental of human institutions, or in other words as representing a basic constitutional order, correlative in importance to individual and public morality.

Since the traditional rites of Confucius's time were clan and family centered, and the family was key to the organization of both economic (primarily agricultural) and religious life in ancient China, Confucius, in the statement above, was identifying as fundamental to human governance key factors in the family-centered life of the agricultural community, and giving them priority over laws imposed from above by conquest regimes, whose dictates, backed by the threat of force, were superimposed on the life of the more consensual agrarian society. In other words, in the Confucian view a large sphere of social activity was to be governed by voluntary adherence to the traditional rites, without the intervention of the state and its laws. Theoretically, and to some degree practically, this constituted a sphere of reserved power for non-governmental organizations operating on a familial or communitarian basis.

Among the followers of Confucius who amplified his teachings, Mencius emphasized, between the two components referred to by Confucius, the importance of personal virtue, and Xunzi the importance of rites. Yet Mencius, while stressing personal virtue as the fundament of both rulership and public life, at the same time insisted that virtue, as both he and Confucius understood it in terms of "humaneness" *(ren)*, was not simply an interior sentiment or habit of mind but something that had to be given tangible form in benefits to the people. He specifically stated that benevolent intentions on the part of the ruler were useless if not carried out in the form of the laws, systems or institutions of the sage-kings. As he said, "Today we have rulers with humane hearts and a reputation for humaneness, and yet the people receive no benefit from them, nor can they serve as models for later ages—all because they do not follow the ways of the early [sage-] kings. Therefore it is said: 'To pursue virtue [lit. goodness] alone does not suffice for governance; nor do laws [models] alone suffice for their own execution'" [4a:1]. In other words, for Mencius personal virtue and social institutions are mutually implicated.

In this passage Mencius uses the term *fa* to designate the model institutions of the sage-kings—the term also used to represent "law" as advocated by the Legalists *(fa jia)*. At the same time, the actual institutions that he cites as representative of the humane rule of the sages—the enfeoffment system, the land distribution ("well-field") system, school system, etc. are all institutions identified with and included in the classical ritual texts as "rites." From this we can see that there was a considerable overlap in the conceptions of "rites" and "laws" in Confucian usage, so Mencius was not departing from the essential formula of Confucius in balancing personal virtue with proper corporate or systemic models spoken of either as "rites" or "laws."

The same is also true of Xunzi. Although he elevates the rites almost to the status of a cosmic principle, as the exemplification in human affairs of the ordering process in Heaven and Earth, when it comes to discussing the key institutions of Kingly Rule, he identifies many of the same policies and systems as Mencius himself had recommended and speaks of them in the same terms Mencius did as the *"fa"* of the king, meaning model enactments of the ruler. Moreover, when presenting his most theoretical justification of the rites, Xunzi does so on the basis not of how these may insure or compel conformity with the dictates of the state, but of how they may serve to cultivate, elevate, and refine people's inner feelings. Thus he too, like Mencius, seeks to sustain the dual emphasis on, and thorough coordination of, the inner springs of personal motivation with the rites already spoken of by Confucius as the essential correlate of virtue. Together, self-restraint (especially on the part of the ruling class) and the hierarchical ordering of society on the basis of proper qualitative distinctions, would reduce, if not eliminate, the need to rely on external constraints.

From this it may be seen that, although the modern West almost always speaks of human rights in legal terms, if Confucianism is to be brought into the discussion, one must think first in terms of "rites" and only secondarily in terms of laws. Further, the classic texts refer mainly to rituals of family, clan, school, and state; the sense of the community as intermediary between family and state is weak, and developed only slowly.

Illustrative of the problem is the most famous of Mencius's communitarian models, the "well-field" system, which is predicated on a division in society between a leadership class and the common people. In the well-field model, land is distributed among eight families occupying equal plots of land around a ninth plot in the center, identified as the public plot, the working of which is shared among the eight surrounding families, and the usufruct of which is their contribution to support of the public order (represented by the enfeoffed nobility) and for mutual aid. In this scheme the family plots are identified as "private" *(si)* and the central plot as "public" *(gong)*, but it is significant that "private" here stands for "family" and not "individual," and that Mencius describes this arrangement, not in terms of individual property rights, but as a cooperative community. "When those in a village who hold land in the same well-field befriend one another in their going out and their coming in [i.e. at home and abroad], assist one another in their protection and defense, and sustain one another through illness and distress, the hundred surnames [the people as a whole] will live together in harmony and affection."[1]

Thus private *(si)* is a familial concept, marked by a cooperative spirit that extends into the community or public sphere *(gong)* as a single interdependent continuum; hence "private" and "public" are complementary, not opposed, values. There is an egalitarian spirit, based on the equal provision of the means of subsistence for all and the principle of mutual aid, yet there is also a division of function between a governing or leadership elite and commoners who provide the means of subsistence.

When projected into the very changed circumstances of Imperial China however, Mencius's prescriptive model becomes problematical: it is based on the Zhou enfeoffment system and presumes the existence of an hereditary aristocracy itself rooted in the local soil and operating as "family," so that the whole social order is permeated by family or kinship values—that is, by the intimate associations and personal treatment supposedly characteristic of life in the agricultural village.

Later in the text Mencius characterizes the order that should prevail among "all-under-Heaven" *(tienxia)* as follows: "Everyone knows the common saying: 'All-under-Heaven (humankind), the state, the family.' The state is the basis of all-under-Heaven; the family is the basis of the state; self[-cultivation] is the basis of the family" [4A:5]. Following this is a passage that makes clear how broadly Mencius conceives of the family: "Governance is not difficult if one does not offend the leading families. Whatever commands the admiration of the leading families the whole state will admire, and what the state admires all-under-Heaven will admire. Thus one's virtue and instruction will inundate all within the four seas" [4A:6].

Both of these latter passages assume the same homogeneity and continuity of family structure and values among the different levels of social and political leadership, presuming the existence of a decentralized enfeoffment system in which everyone treats each other as in some sense kin. The question is then how well this family model applies to the situation in the unified empire of the later dynasties, where the enfeoffment system has been abolished and "state" no longer means a noble house (family), but a civil bureaucratic apparatus taking over the space once occupied by the extended "family."

This radical change in the circumstances of political and social life continued to present a dilemma for dedicated Confucians who still believed in family values as the basis of, and model for, human governance, and who also thought of the rites as the ideal form in which Confucian social values should be expressed. In the seventeenth century the orthodox Confucian Lü Liuliang (1629–1683) contested the claim of imperial dynasties to rule on behalf of the human family, insisting that the dynastic system served only the private interests of the imperial household and not the public interest of "all-under-Heaven."

Thus he asserted:

> During the Three Dynasties every measure the sage-kings took to provide for the people's livelihood and maintain the social order, including the enfeoffment, military and penal systems, no matter how minute in detail or long-range their consequences, were only instituted for the sake of all-under-Heaven and their posterity . . . Not a thing was done nor a law enacted simply for the ruler's own enrichment or aggrandizement, nor was their aim in the slightest to secure for their descendants an estate to be held onto forever, for fear of others trying to seize it. Thus in the *Mean (Zhong yong)* was the sages' humaneness acclaimed for the warmth of its earnest solicitude [for the people].
>
> After the Qin and Han [however], even though among the many systems and institutions adopted from time to time there may have been some good ones ostensibly of benefit to the people or enriching the world, the underlying motive in government has been purely selfish and expedient, the fear being that otherwise one might suffer the loss of what belonged to one's family . . .[2]

In other words the family model had been misappropriated by the dynastic system. Lü still believed in the Confucian rites as the norms that should prevail in government, but he could see that the rise of the centralized dynastic system had fundamentally altered the situation as far as the rites were concerned, and especially that the relationship of the ruler and minister—which should have served the public interest, bridging the gap between the ruler and his subjects—had been critically impaired:

> Parting is in accordance with the rite of ruler and minister, not a departure from that relation. It was only in later times, with the abandonment of the enfeoffment system and adoption of

centralized prefectures and counties, that the world came under the control of one ruler and consequently there was "advancement and retirement" [from office] but no parting. When the Qin abandoned the Way, they established the "rite" of honoring the ruler and abasing the minister, and created an unbridgeable gap between the one on high and the other below, giving the ruler complete control over the minister's advancement and retirement, while leaving him nowhere to go. That was when the relation of rightness between ruler and minister underwent a complete change.[3]

In this passage the key phrase is "leaving him [i.e. the minister] nowhere to go." In the pre-Qin period, Mencius had assumed that the minister, if unable conscientiously to serve in a ruler's court, could leave and seek employment elsewhere in the multi-state system of late Zhou China. With the unification under the imperial dynasties, however, that option no longer existed. There was "nowhere else to go" except back home, no other state and no constituency to support one. In fact sometimes dismissed ministers did not even make it back home, either suffering exile or falling victim to assassination along the way.

Here the concept of a civil society becomes pertinent. If there is no longer a relatively decentralized and autonomous "feudal" structure mediating between the family and royal or imperial power, does any other civil infrastructure or middle class emerge to fill this space and provide the same linking or mediating function between family and the imperial house, or is "civil society" represented only by a civil bureaucracy doing the will of an imperial autocrat?

Some perspective on this question is provided by Ambrose King's discussion of the problem of the individual versus the collectivity, which sums up the views on this point of Chinese social scientists over the last half-century:

Confucians classify the human community into three categories: *ji,* the individual; *jia,* the family; and *qun,* the group. For a

Confucian, the emphasis is on the family, and for this reason Confucian ethics have developed an elaborate role system on the family level. Relatively speaking, the Confucian conception of *qun* is the least articulate. It should be pointed out that, conceptually, the family is also a group. For the purpose of analytic distinction, "family" might be termed "familial group," while the *qun* is "nonfamilistic group" or simply "group." Insofar as Confucian theory is concerned, there is no formal treatment of the concept of *qun*. *Qun* remains an elusive and shifting concept. Fei Xiaotong correctly argues that the boundary between *ji* and *qun* is relative and ambiguous; in the Chinese tradition there is no group boundary as such—the outer limit of the group is the vague concept of *tianxia* [i.e., literally, "all-under-Heaven," or the universe].[4]

From this one can see the difficulty of translating Western concepts of "community" or "collectivity" into meaningful Confucian terms or Chinese experience. However, if we are willing to relax our preconceived Western definitions, we can approach the problem as it might be perceived and reconstructed from a Confucian/Chinese perspective.

To start with one must acknowledge that both in theory and historical practice, the Chinese case gives no ready support to the idea of "community" as an organization or infrastructure mediating between individual and state. The *Great Learning*, already cited as a chapter from the *Record of Rites* later incorporated into the Confucian core curriculum, speaks of the process of education as progressing from self-cultivation to regulating the family, ordering the state and bringing peace to the world ("all-under-Heaven"). Here, the conceptual continuum moves directly from family to state, without any infrastructure between, and even the state is thought of, in ritual terms, as the family writ large (masking the actual fact of a strong bureaucratic state). Indeed this paradigm of the *Great Learning* persists so powerfully down into late imperial times that in Zhang Boxing's eighteenth-century anthology of the statecraft writings of Lu Shiyi (1611–1672), both Lu and he ignored the greater complexities of their own age and classified Lu's writings under headings that moved directly from "Self-cultivation and Regulation of the Family" *(Xiushen jijia)* to "Ordering the State and Bringing Peace to the World" *(zhiguo ping tianxia),* subsuming under this latter category Lu's writings on village administration and community organization.[5] In other words, everything beyond the family pertained to the state and empire.

Thus if one wants to link Confucianism with what today is called an Asian "communitarian" point of view, this version translates readily enough into a statist conception (which is no doubt what its proponents have in mind), but not a participatory community or consensual law. If one looks however into Chinese history, one finds other versions and alternative communitarian traditions, the fates of which tell us something about the prospects for a civil society supportive of human rights in China.

In Confucianism, as a scholarly tradition, the relevant infrastructure between family and state is the school. Though we have little more than ritual details as to how schools were organized or conducted in ancient times, we do know that such centers of learning and scholarly discussion existed in the late Zhou period, and that they concerned themselves with political matters. That they had an influence on popular opinion sufficient to disturb rulers is indicated by the following passage from the memorial of Li Si, prime minister of the first unified empire, calling for the suppression of such activity. He told the emperor:

At present Your Majesty possesses a unified empire . . . and has firmly established for yourself a position of sole supremacy. And yet these independent schools, joining with each other, criticize the codes of laws and instructions. Hearing of the promulgation of a decree, they criticize it, each from the standpoint of his own school. At home they disapprove of it in their hearts; going out they criticize it in the thoroughfare. They seek a reputation by discrediting their sovereign; they appear superior by expressing contrary views, and they lead the lowly multitude in the spreading of slander. If such license is not prohibited, the sovereign power will decline above and partisan factions will form below. It would be well to prohibit this.[6]

Some kind of collective action and popular participation is implied here, but it remains unclear to what extent this activity is rooted in stable institutions or is sustained by an extended community that might have survived into the Imperial age. In the latter Han and later in the Song period scholarly protests in public manifest some degree of collegial solidarity among scholars, but these come from groups in a close, and generally dependent, relation to the court, so their dissent is more like an outburst in a domestic dispute than anything suggestive of a sustained critique of state policy by autonomous communities that seek to exert a countervailing influence on the court.

Possibilities for some articulate educated community, with a more popular base and not simply a scholarly one, do present themselves in the Song. Economic growth, rising affluence, and the spread of printing and literacy created a situation in which education might have been expanded, new schools created, and new communitarian groups formed. Zhang Zai's advocacy of a restored well-field community, inspired by models in the ancient ritual texts and referred to, as we have seen, by Mencius, as well as the community compact of Lü Dazhun (to be discussed later) are examples of such. For Confucians, however, a key question would be whether any such new institutions operated consensually, as ritual communities, or whether they served as adjuncts of state power—as laws or systems.

In what follows we shall consider the possibilities for two such institutions, community schools and community compacts, and their outcomes in an environment dominated by a state power structure and by habits of mind strongly oriented towards either service of the family and lineage, at the lower end, or service to the state at the upper. For us further, there would be the question of whether these groups developed a potential for upward, vertical communication between the lower and higher levels, or whether they operated mostly on a local, horizontal plane, without contributing anything to the discussion and formulation of state policy, such as Li Si above reports the schools of the late Zhou and early Qin attempted to do.

4

School and Community

The ideal of universal education is set forth in two classic texts, the *Record of Rites* and the *Rites of Zhou*, generally considered to have been compiled in the Han period. This timing itself renders the "ideal" problematical enough, since apart from the question of their authenticity as actual records of the early Zhou, there is the strong suspicion that their compilers were imagining or projecting a model (even if it were to some degree an anachronistic reconstruction of some earlier precedent) designed somehow to fit Han circumstances—that is, to fit a unified, centralized state. Whatever may have been the case earlier, the mythic model found in these texts was a uniform, pyramidal structure embodying a perfect hierarchy of authority, with the presumption that such authority would be based on a Confucian ordering of ritual values and be exercised in a consensual manner according to Confucian standards of ritual respect.

The Han state, in its centralized structure and bureaucratic mode of operation, stood in some contrast to this notion—a contrast already seen in our earlier reference to the "Evolution of Rites" chapter, which differentiated a primordial, consensual, communal ideal from a later historical stage of competition for power and profit. Indeed this ambiguity and tension between the primitive communal ideal and the realities of the Han state is reflected in the alternative title by which the *Rites of Zhou (Zhouli)* itself was known: the *Institutes or Offices of Zhou (Zhou guan)*. The latter bureaucratic title suggests how the Confucian model was modified and construed to fit the Han state structure, which was the product of a very different Legalist ideology, in which the public interest *(gong)* was identified with the state *(guan)*.

In later historical fact, both of these ritual texts were claimed as models by reformers, at least professedly Confucian, whose aims might nevertheless range over a wide spectrum from the decentralized communitarian mode to policies favoring strong state action and control. Among Song Confucians both types were represented, and educational issues could be contested from either side. The difference between them, however, was not over the unitary ideal, but only on how that unity could best be achieved. It was not a question of a radical pluralism versus a unified overall authority, but how legitimate superior authority could be exercised while respecting and reconciling a diversity of needs and views. Confucius had expressed this in the *Analects* as achieving harmony without uniformity *(he er bu tong)*, unity without total conformity.[1]

Within this general spectrum, proposals were made in the Song to institute universal education, and at least three efforts were made by the government to establish a country-wide school system under the leadership of Fan Zhongyan (989–1052), Wang Anshi (1021–1086) and Cai Jing (1046–1126). Little came of these ideas owing to the political eclipse of their sponsors and the military setbacks of the Song, but the ideal of universal schooling was sustained partly by the importance given it in the text of *Mencius,* a prime source for Confucian reformism in the Song, as well as by the classic ritual texts just cited.

Mencius had talked about the ruler's responsibility to provide first for the people's material welfare, through the system of equal landholding in well-field communities, and then of providing schools for all—a natural enough idea for Confucians, who believed that good government depended on education, not laws and punishments. In Neo-Confucian political thought this combination of well-field community and community school was to become emblematic of the Confucian ideal and of the goal of political reformism in later ages, since it expressed in institutional form the values of economic equality and education for all as the basis for meritocratic advancement into the public service for some, if not a more civilized life for society as a whole.

Zhu Xi (1130–1200), who became the supreme intellectual authority of the Neo-Confucian movement in the late Song and after, in his preface to the *Great Learning*, first among the neo-canonical Four Books, spoke of the ancient sage-kings' provision for schools from the capital city down to the village level. It is important to note here that he referred specifically to the "village" and not just to "local" in general, and that he spoke of "schools" as actual physical structures, not just to schooling or education in general, which could just as well have been provided by instruction in the home of the parent or tutor—a more normal thing in traditional China. These were to be schools that, on the one hand, extended education beyond the family, clan, or lineage, but on the other hand, would provide higher education within a local setting—that is, intermediate between the family and the level of higher central administration. Further, in a preface to his *Reflections on Things at Hand (Jinsilu)*, Zhu's expansion and philosophical updating of the *Great Learning*, he also spoke of this book as providing a basis for the self-cultivation and self-education of boys in remote villages who were without teachers. From this we know that Zhu had in mind an educational curriculum and institutional system for education on the village level.

Since Zhu Xi, during his own lifetime, was not, for the most part, in favor at court, and even suffered political persecution in his last years, these ideas, not withstanding Zhu's immense intellectual and moral authority among scholars, were not put into effect. In any case, worsening conditions under the Song would have rendered their accomplishment difficult.

Remarkably enough, however, an unexpected opportunity arose under the succeeding Mongol dynasty, the Yuan, when the Grand Khan Khubilai had among his key civil advisors Xu Heng (1209–1281), a convert to Zhu Xi's teachings. Xu, in his famous Five Point Memorial to Khubilai of 1266, recommended the Mongol ruler's adoption of Han Chinese policies of civil administration, and concluded with two points stressed by Mencius and Zhu Xi: policies favoring agriculture (something the Mongols had little experience with) and the setting up of local schools. Khubilai approved these, and put Xu Heng in charge of the educational program, but though Xu was able to install a new Neo-Confucian curriculum at the capital, which thereafter became the standard for China and subsequently for all East Asia, the program for local schools languished, no doubt because Khubilai's priorities for resource allocation, and those of local officials, lay elsewhere.

The issue came up again in 1313 under Emperor Renzong, when the Minister of Agriculture Zhang Wenqian, a student and protege of Xu Heng, recalled this item of unfinished business at court and urged that steps be taken to implement it. Again authorization was given, but, significantly, its execution—the creation of a system of community schools *(shexue)*—was left to the Ministry of Agriculture, subsequently known as the Ministry of Agricultural Households *(hubu,* a title which in Zhou times had served as an alternate for the Ministry of Education, but for which the standard translation into English later was "Ministry of Revenue.")[2] From this one can see that the primary function of the ministry was to extract revenue from the agricultural sector. That being the case, one can further imagine how, for all of Minister Zhang's original good intentions to educate farmers, the educational priority would suffer a far from benign neglect in the hands of revenue agents. A leading contemporary historian Yu Ji (1272–1348) commented ruefully on the neglect of education by local officials: "These days local officials are so pressed and preoccupied with fiscal and judicial duties that they do not have the time to attend to basic governance, much less to education!"[3]

The significance of the term *shexue* for "community school" lies first in *she*, which suggests a corporate body with religious roots in the local soil, and then in *xue* for "learning," the process by which one could become literate and articulate enough to participate in a higher culture, thereby acquiring the potential for engaging in the upper levels of society and government long dominated by literati. Traditionally, according to the paradigm of the *Great Learning*, the aim of Confucian education was to move from the properly centered self to higher and wider concentric circles of social service. But whether in fact a system of community schools could have achieved that level of popular participation in governance, or contributed to that goal, is the question here.

As actually carried out, this system involved only part-time, off-season, instruction for the moral uplift of farmers in local communities, and differed markedly from the full-time instruction in classical studies conducted under the supervision of the Ministry of Rites in state schools (county and above) for prospective recruits into the bureaucracy. Such a bifurcation in schooling was not what either Zhu Xi or Xu Heng had had in mind, but at least the community school kept alive the ideal of education for all.

The next important episode in this conflicted history of community schools comes from the first Ming reign and the dynasty's founder, Emperor Ming Taizu. As a self-educated peasant with a commoner's (rather than a scholar's) concern for popular uplift, but no doubt also with the prompting of his own Neo-Confucian advisors, quite familiar with Zhu Xi's ideas, Ming Taizu ordered the establishment of community schools throughout the land, aware that something of the sort had been adopted under the Mongols. Later, in article 32 of his "Placard for People's Instruction," in 1398, he referred to this earlier initiative as follows:

In the Yuan dynasty, many village children attended school. In the early years of the Hongwu period villages everywhere were ordered to establish community schools *(shexue)* to instruct the children in good conduct. Incompetent officials and *lijia* took advantage of this to indulge in corrupt practices. The children of families with adult males obviously had the spare time to attend school, but the officials took bribes and excused them from attending school. Nevertheless the children of families without adult males who had no spare time to attend school, were forced to go to school. This caused hardship for the people. Therefore, the community schools were abolished. From now on, the children of the common people, regardless of their location and number, shall be instructed by virtuous persons. The schools shall open early in the tenth month and close at the end of the twelfth month each year. If families with many adult males have enough spare time, they may have their children continually engaged in study. Those officials, functionaries and *lijia* who dare to interfere with them shall be punished severely.[4]

This short article has at least two major significances: it marked the effective privatization of schooling on the village level, with the consequence that only children of the well-to-do, or their special proteges, would engage in regular study that might prepare them for higher learning, while most commoners, engaged in agriculture and handicrafts, would get minimal off-season instruction if any. The effect of the foregoing was to create two different levels of education—one administered through the Ministry of Revenue on the local level, and the other by the Ministry of Rites, leading up to official recruitment. Administratively then what had once been envisaged by Neo-Confucians as a single system of general education had become bifurcated into two: one below the county level, largely privatized but retaining a ritual of the Six Maxims for public moral uplift; and the other for the elite, oriented towards the civil service. Alongside this, of course, were the private academies increasingly the focus of serious scholarly study and discussion, largely maintained by local support of the educated elite but increasingly, in late Imperial times, directed towards achieving success in the civil service examinations. In other words, it led to the neglect of general education on the level of the local rice-roots community, to the increasing bifurcation of education between rudimentary instruction in family, clan, or lineage settings on the lower level, and to elite classical learning oriented towards state service or rarified classical research at the upper level. Little of this served to bridge the gap between local autonomy and central authority. As a consequence in modern studies when reference is made to "local education" it typically relates to the lower levels of central administration (the county or sub-prefecture), and rarely has to do with the village community except in connection with family, clan, or lineage, or with private academies that moved to fill this gap in public schooling on the intermediate level.

During the early Ming there seems to have been a significant growth of community schools as local elites and magistrates, in a period of relative stability, attempted to implement the general intent of Ming Taizu's policy to encourage local education. In the longer run, however, it proved difficult to sustain this growth and even to maintain existing schools. Chen Xianzhang (1428–1500), Wang Yangming, and Li Mengyang (1473–1529) are among the notable scholars who sought to restore or promote community schools in the face of their serious deterioration.[5] The actual situation varied greatly from place to place but as Ho Ping-ti (He Bingdi) characterized the situation, "In the long run, many community schools became derelict, owing either to chronic financial difficulties or to the decline of official or community zeal."[6] In the midst of what he calls "the general negligence of the late Ming period," some of the educational need (as noted above) was met by the "private" or local academies, at least among the members of, or aspirants to, the elite (a development to which we shall return later), but this did little to improve the situation among the rural population at large. Thus, as a more recent study has put it, the situation at the end of the Ming was marked by: "The state's inability and unwillingness to overcome the first difficulties of the system, and the apparently peripheral role and discontinuous existence of the schools in various localities."[7]

In the Qing essentially the same pattern obtained. While community schools existed, they were often maintained by local elites and lineages on a "private" (i.e. family) basis, similar to "charity schools" *(yixue)*, an arrangement that, if it did not serve the purpose primarily of advancing their members into the ranks of the official elite, provided only a minimal literacy to commoners, insufficient for their significant participation in civic affairs on a policy-making level. In the words of a Qing official writing in 1699, describing the replacement of community schools by charity schools: "At the present time youngsters of rich and powerful families are taught by private tutors who are engaged by these families. Those of poor and lowly families cannot study for lack of financial support. But local authorities look on education as something non-essential and superfluous, not to be undertaken with limited resources, so the ancient community school system *(shexue)* cannot be revived."[8]

In a similar vein William Rowe speaks of the efforts by the leading official and educator Chen Hongmou in southwest China: "In settling on *yixue* [charity schools] rather than *shexue* [community schools] as the term for the new Yunnan schools, it seems that Chen and his superiors were attempting to draw on the community-sponsorship elements of the *shexue* tradition but emphasizing more than had Zhu Xi and Lü Kun [see next page] the elements of standardization, orthodoxy and equalization of opportunity, all under state supervision."[9] The situation has been characterized more generally by Evelyn Rawski as follows:

The community schools *(shexue)* of the Ming, like their Qing counterparts, were charitable elementary schools established in towns and villages on local initiative with the state's blessing. One study shows that there were 3837 *shexue* in 472 Ming administrative units, or an average of slightly more than eight schools per unit. *These schools provided education for only a small proportion of the school-age population* [italics mine]. In Ming and Qing times, most boys were educated in lineage schools, village schools (where tuition had to be paid), and private schools in the households of the well-to-do. Since the records that would enable us to evaluate the extent of private schooling are rare and scattered, quantitative estimates of the rate of school attendance are at best speculative. Elsewhere I have calculated that there were enough private and charitable schools by the late Qing to teach basic literacy to between one-third and one-half the males of school age.[10]

If the foregoing represents the dominant pattern and course of education, a significant side-current continued in the advocacy of community schools and their attempted implementation by individual scholar-officials educated in Zhu Xi's curriculum and familiar with Neo-Confucian precedents in the matter of community schools. Whether as influential writers or as independent-minded officials, they kept this educational ideal alive in the sixteenth, seventeenth and eighteenth centuries as what might be called a scholarly sub-tradition struggling to make itself heard. Generally these efforts were in close ideological association with the practice of community granaries, community compacts, and community wine-drinking ceremonies, as well as other measures of local organization and popular moral uplift recommended by Zhu Xi.

A prime example of such advocacy—though by no means the only one—was Lü Kun (1536–1618). Respected as a conscientious and effective local administrator, on his own he promoted community schools and wrote much on educational matters, often in the colloquial language in order to reach a larger popular audience (one aspect of a wider movement towards the popularization of learning in the sixteenth century).[11] Lü's *Records of*

Practical Administration (Shi zheng lu) was used as a model in the Qing dynasty; he was canonized in the Confucian temple in 1826 and was also held in high respect by Japanese scholars of the Tokugawa and Meiji periods.

In an essay on "The Restoration of Community Schools," Lü commented on both the deterioration of education on the local level, and the neglect of general public education in official schools, whose teachers emphasized only literary skills useful in civil service examinations. Consequently, the farming population developed an aversion to this kind of study. They saw in it no tangible benefit to compensate for the loss of able-bodied manpower at home and in the fields—an endemic problem already encountered in Ming Taizu's initial effort to set up community schools. Lü said:

> Regarding the restoration of the community schools for the nurturing of uneducated children, nothing is more urgent for the realization of [Mencius's] "kingly way" than to educate the common people, and for the nourishing of moral uprightness nothing should take precedence over training for the very young. [As things stand today] it is long since proper schooling has been carried out and one cannot expect much from local teachers: one can only do something about the matter of community schools . . .
>
> Ever since true education has declined, the whole world has ceased to understand what true learning is all about. For over two thousand years it has been misconceived, and right down to the present time what teachers have told their disciples and parents have transmitted to their sons has only been that they should come first in the [civil service] examinations as a stepping stone to wealth and rank . . .
>
> The best thing in the world is for young people to study, whether they do so for the lofty goal of achieving good report and accomplishing great deeds, or for the more modest goal of recognizing characters and understanding their meanings (i.e. for basic literacy) . . .
>
> The official in charge should proclaim to the common people:

"Hereafter children of an age to study are to be sent to community schools; even if they are poor and needed for work at home, they should [at least] attend school after the tenth month [harvest] and only return to their homes after the third month [for planting]. If after three years of schooling their talents prove to be such that nothing more can be expected of them, let them return to their usual occupations . . ."[12]

From this brief passage one can see the factors Lü had to contend with in his attempt to "restore community schools," which for him represented an ancient ideal badly neglected and only fitfully practiced in imperial times. By necessity he appealed for this restoration of schooling—outside the home but below the county level—to be undertaken by local officials; there was no other class or natural constituency to whom he could readily turn for this initiative and leadership responsibility. Second, he was aware that the dominance of this same class and its official culture presented a problem in that preparation for the examinations and bureaucratic success dominated the educational scene. Despite these obstacles, however, he insisted that general education would be indispensable to public morality and a sound polity, even while he realized that he had to contend with over "two thousand years" of misconceived and misguided education, during which time worthy Confucian predecessors of his had carried on a long, losing struggle to remedy it. No doubt Lü had in mind the example of Confucius himself, who kept trying to change things despite his own evident lack of success, and he was mindful too of the persistent idealism of Zhu Xi, who, while acknowledging that "the Way has not prevailed for over two thousand years," continued to hope for its realization.

One of Lü's successors in this struggle was Chen Hongmou (1696–1771), a distinguished provincial governor of the Qing dynasty notable for his practical statecraft. An avowed latter-day disciple of Zhu Xi, he was also an admirer of Lü Kun and included some of Lü's essays in a compendium of important writings on education that became a standard reference work in the Qing. Chen deplored both the cultivation of literary skills at a premium in the examination culture and the kind of antiquarian classical research pursued by the so-called Han Learning or Evidential Learning in his day. Instead he promoted "substantial" or "practical" learning *(shixue)*, which included moral instruction and basic education for the general population, not excepting non-Chinese minorities in frontier areas where he served. Chen wrote:

> Human nature is essentially good. There is no one who cannot be civilized and enlightened. Chinese and barbarians are essentially the same . . . It is the duty of those who hold local authority to ensure that schools are established in each locality, to see that these do not fall into neglect after they are established, and to make sure that they do not exist only on paper . . .
>
> Local officials are charged with shepherding the people and providing moral guidance to them. The goal must be to extend education to every locality . . . to the end that there be educated persons everywhere, and education be underway in every remote village and marketplace . . .
>
> The way of shepherding the people involves no more than educating and nourishing them . . . By "nourishing" I mean construction and maintenance of irrigation works, encouragement of land reclamation and patronage of community granaries . . . By education I mean promoting civilized behavior, diligently managing public schools and widely distributing classic texts.

Like Lü Kun, Chen believed that this kind of general education should be available to women:

> There is no uneducable person in the world, and no person whom it is justifiable to leave uneducated. How then can female children alone be excepted? . . . The view that female children need not be educated is a violation of principle and an affront to the Way . . . A worthy wife becomes a worthy mother and a

worthy mother will have worthy sons and grandsons. Thus the process of civilization begins in the women's quarters, and the fortunes of the entire household rest on the pillar of its womenfolk. Hence the education of women is a matter of the greatest importance.[13]

From the examples of Lü Kun in the Ming and Chen Hongmou in the Qing, we can see that there was a tradition continuing from Zhu Xi of Neo-Confucian concern with general education on the level of the local community, recognizing the need for education of the population as a whole, and not just of the elite in schools supported by lineages, local gentry, or the state bureaucracy. Moreover, these schools were conceived as part of a local community infrastructure including community granaries and community compact organizations that would serve public needs beyond the level of family and clan. In both cases, however, Lü and Chen acknowledge and fundamentally criticize an educational establishment oriented more to service of the state than to the advancement of humane Confucian learning for all.

In conclusion something should be said about the local academies *(shu yuan)*, which played a large role in the rise of the Neo-Confucian reform movement, independent of the state school system. In fact, it was through the academies that the Neo-Confucian School of the Way got its start, long before the new teaching became established in official schools, and academies continued to be especially active in the Yuan and Ming periods as centers of the intellectual, social, and even ritual life of the local gentry. Generally started by local initiative and sustained, through periodic phases of decline and revival, by local support, the academies have sometimes been distinguished from state schools by the prefix "private." If this were appropriate, it would have to be in the sense of private and public as complementary, and not as in opposition, nor in the sense that "private" meant independent of official support, which was rarely the case.

Academies were usually glad to receive recognition in the form of imperial inscriptions and gifts, and officials often patronized them.

It is true that their members thought of academies as voluntary and relatively autonomous organizations. Zhu Xi, who greatly encouraged academies, particularly emphasized the importance of their voluntary nature, and in formulating a kind of charter for the famous White Deer Grotto Academy at Lushan, he added a postscript emphasizing that its members should not think of themselves as subject to school rules or regulations but as voluntary subscribers to, and self-disciplined participants in, the upholding of shared values.[14]

Alas for Zhu Xi's good intentions, most academies ignored his abjuration of rules, and even those that adopted Zhu's "precepts" or "articles" often called them "rules." This indicates the prevalent conception of academies as adjunct to and generally homologous with an authoritarian established order. During the mid to late Ming period academies did become important centers of intellectual discussion *(jiangxue)*, and even promoted active discussion of public issues, but after the official suppression of such political criticism at the end of the sixteenth century, they ceased significantly to exercise this function of a public forum.

In the following passages Thomas H. C. Lee evaluates the potential of these local academies as centers for what might be called a civil society in the public sphere:

> The beginning of *shuyuan* was during a time of political turmoil, when the center was lost. The only viable social organization, namely, the family, very naturally responded to the educational need of society and the *shuyuan* was the product. It was in this sense that academies were private. In restoring the famous Bailudong Academy, Zhu Xi continued the rhetoric, but infused a significantly original dimension into *shuyuan* education in that he articulated a role for the newly risen local *shiren*. His idea was to incorporate the educated elite, the literati, in and out of

office, into the state and local-community continuum, so that through *shuyuan* (and selected local organizations) the intellectuals could mediate between the potentially conflicting extremes . . .

During Mongol rule, paradoxically because of the lack of effective local administration, Chinese society was able to consolidate its local community identity, and the result was a greater opportunity for academies to grow . . . Although one should not equate the strengthening of local self-government (however inadequate, and unarticulated) with what a modern interpreter would understand as the formation of "civil society" . . . still, the Confucian notion of local communality and the conviction that moral autonomy was the ultimate value did prepare Chinese intellectuals to exercise their absolutist search for truth, often conducted in local educational institutions (notably the academies), and from time to time did help them to achieve the purpose of what a modern "public sphere" is supposed to achieve . . .[15]

Later in the Qing period, while local academies did serve to generate some discussion of public issues, their educational functions became increasingly directed towards preparation of students to take the civil service examination. Academies receded in importance as centers of political activism, while lineage organizations, working to advance themselves within the imperial system, flourished in relative harmony with that system in contrast to the state's distrust of more broad-based, non-kin, communitarian institutions like the academies, seen as centers of potential opposition.[16] Ron Guey Chu, who presents an eloquent case for the survival of public discussion in the early Qing period by leading scholars who survived from the late Ming, nevertheless concedes that its political role was increasingly attenuated—that "dissenting intellectuals could not bring their opposition to bear on real politics in the longer run" and were "unable to establish more permanent locally-based institutions to effect long-term change."[17]

Likewise William Rowe speaks of academies in Qing China as ceasing to perform any independent role: "By imperial mandate, Qing *shu yuan* followed the earlier experience of prefectural and county schools: bureaucratization of management, formalization of curricula, and gradual emasculation as centers of independent scholarly inquiry."[18]

Meanwhile, those engaged in classical scholarly research could bring classical precedents to bear on policy issues, but their statecraft concerns either fell within the scope of the established imperial structure or, if they went beyond this, lacked a constituency among the educated elite large or powerful enough to achieve the major systemic changes needed to reform a lethargic and often corrupt mandarinate.[19] This is not to deny that the academy did serve an important function in nurturing individual self-cultivation, as has been emphasized in recent studies of pedagogy in academies of the lower Yangtze valley,[20] yet however much this contributed to individual "self-strengthening" it could still be dismissed later by the Communist leader Liu Shaoqi as essentially individualistic and idealistic, rather than engaged with pressing social and political issues. The plausibility of Liu's criticism (though not its validity—see chapter 8) is vouched for by a strong proponent of government reform in the late Qing, Fang Dongshu (1772–1851), who lamented the lack in his own time (the mid-nineteenth century) of the public debate that had been engendered by the academies of the sixteenth century. This lament underscored the fact that, while the academies had had the potential for airing critical issues and might have served the "amphibious" function of bridging the communication gap between local society and central policy-making on major public issues, they were unable to sustain it. Such an outcome is not mainly attributable to continuing persecution or repression, but to the fact that the academies themselves, while remaining essentially local and relatively autonomous, still participated in the larger culture, polishing the literary skills of those who competed in the civil service examinations. Thus they served the upward mobility of the educated elite more than they served the need for general education or provided a public forum on major policy questions.

To say this is not to imply that the reformism of a Fang Dongshu was wholly in vain. Fang's call for a revival of Donglin-type advocacy did more than simply lament its atrophy in the early and mid-Qing period. It kept alive in unfavorable circumstances a tradition of such advocacy until, in the mid- and late nineteenth century, the worsening crises of the Qing allowed new voices to articulate the need for public criticism in a more radical form—the "pure criticism" or "Voices of Remonstrance" *(qingi)*.[21] This, in turn, as we shall see in chapter 6, contributed to Liang Qichao's sense at the turn of the century that China had a prime need for precisely such communitarian institutions to promote the discussion of public issues.

Meanwhile, the Ming, starting with Ming Taizu himself, had attempted to fill the educational need by promoting another system of public instruction, the community compact *(xiangyue)*, which is the subject of the next chapter.

5

The Community Compact

In the absence of more public schooling the community compact *(xiangyue)* was one of the key instruments by which Zhu Xi sought to promote popular education and moral uplift among the people. For many later scholars Zhu's advocacy of the community compact had an importance at least equal to that of his philosophical ideas, and for historians too it has proved of major significance—though not necessarily of a kind Zhu Xi would have appreciated. Resorted to again and again in different societies, places, and times in East Asia, the community compact endured into the twentieth century. Moreover it was closely linked to a set of other prototypical Neo-Confucian institutions—community granaries, self-defense units, local schools and academies, family rituals, community wine-drinking ceremonies, etc.—that served as models for a local infrastructure in late Imperial China and Yi dynasty Korea. Further, though the *xiangyue* was not an original conception of Zhu Xi's, its coming to prominence—indeed its being rescued from oblivion—is attributable almost entirely to Zhu Xi's celebration of its distinctive features, which, through many historical vicissitudes, exerted a continuing appeal. Finally, the very checkered and conflicted history of the community compact itself illustrates perhaps better than does any other local institution the persistent tension between Neo-Confucian communitarian ideas and Chinese imperial rule.

In an earlier book, *The Liberal Tradition in China*,[1] I highlighted the less well recognized "liberal" features of Zhu's community compact, pointing first to his efforts at popular uplift on the local level through his proclamations to the people. Typical of this genre was Zhu's proclamation in Zhangzhou (1190–1191), the most notable feature of which was Zhu's emphasis on mutuality, reciprocity, and cooperation among community members. These values, rather than the imposition of superior power or punitive law, were to be the basis for the proper conduct of public affairs on the village level. Here the appeal was to a combination of self-respect and mutual regard among persons as the natural means of upholding a voluntaristic social order, which was seen as preferable to any enforcement of state control from above.[2]

These values that Zhu promoted through the medium of his public proclamations were also built into the community compact *(xiangyue)*, which Zhu Xi adapted from a follower of Cheng Yi, Lü Dajun, as the basic "constitution" for a self-governing community. As I said in *The Liberal Tradition*, the ideal of voluntary cooperation that inspired this system is expressed in the term *yue*, a compact or contract entered into by members of a community for their mutual benefit. Most notable is the personalistic character of the contract, which places a stronger emphasis on mutual respect for the needs and aspirations of persons than on respect for property rights or an exact quid-pro-quo in the exchange of goods.

The main provisions of this compact called for mutual encouragement in the performance of worthy deeds, mutual admonition in the correction of errors and failings, reciprocal engagement in rites and customs, and mutual aid in times of distress and misfortune. Under each of these headings there were detailed specifications of the kinds of actions for which members of the compact took personal responsibility. There was also provision for the rotation of leadership within the group for carrying out the terms of the compact.

Here then was a model for popular education in direct relation to the daily life of the community, a practical way of implementing basic Neo-Confucian principles in a context wider than kinship or personal relations. At a time that witnessed the steady extension and aggrandizement of state power, Zhu was not content simply to let public morality depend on the discipline of family life alone, or even the five-family units of local security organization *(wubao)*, but sought to incorporate the principle of voluntarism into community structures that might mediate between state power and family interests. Thus he recommended a social program on the basis of which one could limit the intervention of the state in local affairs, and share authority among more autonomous local units, relying on popular education and ritual observance as an alternative to punitive law. Underlying this program was the idea of personal self-transformation and communal cooperation as the basis of the polity, i.e., the fusion of public and private interests *(gongsi yiti)*. Other expressions of this attitude are to be found in types of local instruction based on Zhu Xi's own proclamations; in the community granaries to which Zhu devoted much attention as a local official; and in the so-called Family Ritual of Zhu Xi.

Zhu's treatment of these matters was extraordinarily detailed, showing a fine grasp of practical administration. It is not surprising that they should have become models for the implementation of his teachings in later times. Because these most authentic of Neo-Confucian institutions had their importance on the local level, however, often escaping the attention of modern scholars preoccupied with affairs of the Imperial Court and state, their significance has not always been appreciated.[3]

Subsequently at a 1984 conference on Neo-Confucian education, Robert Hymes and Monika Ubelhör offered significant amendments to what I had said in *The Liberal Tradition*. Discussing Zhu Xi's perception of the need for some public infrastructure between family and state, Hymes noted Zhu Xi's aim to incorporate the principle of voluntarism into "community structures that might mediate between state power and family interests," after which he raised questions about seeing this as a response to "the steady extension and aggrandizement of state power" in Zhu's own time. Hymes went on to say:

> The memory of an expansionist state—the memory of the failed reforms and the factional excesses of Wang Anshi and of the vigorous centralization and equally vigorous persecutions of the dictator Cai Jing—unquestionably lay behind the community-based voluntarism of Zhu Xi and other Southern Song Neo-Confucians. But the state that faced them in their own time, far from extending its power and control, had been so weakened by the wars of the Northern Song/Southern Song transition and by the enormous burden of maintaining border armies against the Jin that it found itself less and less able to gather revenue and perform the basic function of maintaining order in the localities. It had effectively withdrawn from any serious attempts to influence from the center the welfare of rural communities . . . The state's failures and its partly deliberate withdrawal left a gap into which local gentlemen (and not-so-gentle men) moved. I would suggest that one may see the community compact, too, as an attempt to fill this gap . . . Neo-Confucian reformers in Southern Song built their new non-state institutions in the space left by the failure: the space, to return to de Bary's formulation, "between state power and family interests."[4]

This is an important amendment to my description of the Song situation, which was unduly abbreviated, conflating the rather different circumstances in which Lu Dajun's compact had been put forward in the eleventh century and those to which Zhu Xi later responded in the twelfth—important because in the subsequent history of the community compact, as it was repeatedly resurrected, either one of these contrasting circumstances could figure in the process—at times it could involve the attempted extension of state power or resistance to the same, and at other times it could reflect the deterioration of central control, which left a vacuum to be filled on the local level.

Monika Ubelhör's study compared the original text of the Lü family compact with Zhu Xi's later adaptation of it, pointing out significant differences as well as similarities in both text (including classical textual precedents) and social context. Among these features the following are relevant here:

1. The Song compacts, sometimes thought to have the *Rites of Zhou* as their inspiration, shared with the latter a common emphasis on mutual assistance, but in contrast to the *Zhouli* were "voluntary, locally initiated, and not centrally presented associations." They also emphasized the effort of "individual members to work for improvement in their daily conduct"—"one of the most salient features of the Lü compact . . . absent in the *Rites of Zhou*."[5]

2. From letters of Lü Dazhun, Ubelhör concludes that such voluntary associations were already coming into being in the eleventh century through the efforts of the common people in Lü's native region, and that Lü attempted to assert Confucian leadership in local communities at that time—"an attempt well in tune with one major trend of his time . . . in which a decidedly Neo-Confucian elite with new elan set out to take the lead in all walks of life and to wrest from other social forces the influence which they had held for centuries in Chinese society."[6]

In this connection it is worth noting that what constituted the elite in Zhu's mind was their moral and cultural qualifications. He is quite pointed in predicating seniority, wisdom and experience, and self-disciplined decorum as the qualities that merit respect in this hierarchy, not entitlements of rank and wealth.[7]

3. "Neither Lü Dazhun's nor Zhu Xi's compacts represent fluent attempts at indoctrination; rather they aim at bringing to life the moral potential of the compact members. In this respect each version relies mainly . . . on voluntary means of bringing about a harmonious social order . . . At the same time, Zhu Xi's version seems to have been inspired by a strong sense of the need for a hierarchical structuring of society and a belief in the gentle

but irresistible force of ritually conducted communal ceremonies. In the end Zhu Xi's compact was directed at the same practical results as the Lü version, that is, harmoniously ordered communities that provided for the needs of all its members."[8]

At this point we do well to remember that it was Zhu Xi who saw in the Lü compact an instrument for achieving his aim of building a well-ordered, self-sustaining, and relatively autonomous local community. Zhu conceived of his own efforts to define the leadership responsibilities of the educated elite as sub-serving the needs of the entire community on the basis of a voluntary participation of all its members in a single consensual association, embracing all classes. This point is underscored in the aforementioned public proclamations of Zhu Xi as a local administrator, wherein the basic values and practices upheld are addressed to elite and commoner alike *(quanyu shimin)*, rather than being directed to one or the other alone. Thus the basic precepts proposed for the compacts are the same as those found in Zhu's Zhangzhou proclamation of 1190.[9] It is this same consistency of approach that led later proponents of community compacts to identify the Lü Family version with Zhu Xi's, considering them as essentially one and the same. As Ubelhör states, "The particular focus of Zhu Xi's version of the compact . . . served to promote and often passed under the name of the Lü compact."[10]

We may sum up the key aims of the Zhu–Lü compact as the establishment of stable self-regulating local communities through the leadership of an educated moral elite that encouraged self-discipline, mutual respect and assistance, voluntary efforts, and joint rituals to provide for the needs of the community as a whole. This fits, I believe, with my earlier characterization of the community compact as part of a "liberal" Neo-Confucian program in the context of twelfth-century Song China. Admittedly its elite aspect will raise questions in some modern minds, but perhaps no more so than does a comparable aspect of early twentieth-century Western liberalism, in the view of the British classicist Gilbert Murray, who saw modern liberalism as the outcome of a Western development from classical Greek and Roman antecedents through medieval and Renaissance humanism into its modern form. Murray described this outcome as, "The product of a leisured and in some ways privileged class, working to extend its own privileges to wider and wider circles, aiming at freedom of thought and discussion, and equally pursuing the free exercise of individual conscience and promotion of the common good."[11]

The question that naturally arises at this juncture is whether, in the Chinese case, there was any comparable development out of this Neo-Confucian "liberalism" towards some approximation of the Western variety. To address the question most directly I turn to the very different form of community compact prevalent in late Qing China at a time when enterprising members of the Western elite, more expansive and expansionist by far than the Confucian elite, came to encounter the latter on their own home grounds.

When one tries to find the Qing dynasty equivalent of the community compact *(xiangyue)*, one immediately runs into a confusion of terms. By this time the original meaning of the term *xiangyue* had become obscured because the practice itself had become largely lost. The expression *xiangyue* still existed, but it had come to be thought of as an empty ritual and sometimes lecture, variously pedantic or popular, on the so-called *Sacred Edict* of the Kangxi emperor (r. 1662–1722) in one of its more or less elaborate, formulaic versions. A typical account of the *xiangyue* by a modern Chinese scholar conveys the sense of its practice as essentially a routine exercise in which the local gentry made obeisance to imperial ideology:

> Since the early Qing, there was the enforcement of the semi-monthly expounding of the sixteen politico-moral maxims of the *Sacred Edict* intended to indoctrinate the masses with the

official ideology. In this process of indoctrination, the gentry were requested to give their assistance. This is substantiated by the following passage: "On the first and fifteenth day of a month, *zhou* and *xian* magistrates should lead educational officials and assisting officials to public meeting places, gather the soldiers and the people, and explain to them the *Sacred Edict*."[12]

The largely mechanical character, as well as the generally stultifying atmosphere of this required ritual, is conveyed by further references to its practice in the late nineteenth century. Nevertheless, "in the nineteenth century some magistrates still seriously observed this semimonthly ceremony and personally led in the discussion of these maxims. Some magistrates required candidates of examinations to write the maxims from memory. On some occasions, elderly licentiates *(shengyuan)* were recommended to take charge of the expounding of the maxims in the countryside."[13]

By this time the *xiangyue* had become thoroughly identified with lectures on the *Sacred Edict* that took place in various locales and centers of gentry activity, stressing the "gentry's duties of loyalty and service to the government and its laws":

The same purpose of indoctrination was served by the Sixteen Maxims of the *Sacred Edict,* which were issued in 1670 and further amplified in 1724. Among the maxims were these: "Keep the school in high regard in order to direct the scholar's conduct." "Denounce heretical sayings in order to exalt the orthodox doctrines." The Hanlin Academy was ordered to write a rhymed essay on the maxim of denouncing heretical sayings; this essay was to be distributed to all schools for recitation so that "good customs would be formed and the people's hearts rectified." The whole tenor of the Sixteen Maxims stresses obedience and submissiveness. Semimonthly meetings were held in the schools at which these maxims were expounded. In the nineteenth century, when these meetings were not always held regularly, imperial edicts urged the observance of this ceremony . . . Even the provincial director-of-studies, on arriving in a locality to give an examination, was first to expound the orthodox teachings to the students so that they would know "which direction to follow." So indoctrinated, the students could then be used to preach these maxims to the population at large.[14]

It would not be difficult to cite other modern observers who report on these ritual lectures and the *Sacred Edict* in the same vein. Indeed so commonplace has this view become that the stereotype is as much of a fixture in the minds of contemporary historians as the ritual itself had become in the Qing period, without anyone's thinking to ask about the original significance of the term *xiangyue*, which in its literal meaning does not convey any necessary connection with a *Sacred Edict* or a lecture on the same.

I now take a shortcut to a recent study, Victor Mair's "Language and Ideology in the Written Popularizations of the *Sacred Edict*,"[15] which focuses on the so-called *Sacred Edict* and its "popularization" in the vernacular. As the discussion proceeds it will be necessary to consider the contents of the Sixteen Maxims that constitute the message to be communicated to the populace at large, and to see how these contents compare with earlier versions. Therefore I reproduce them in the form they are presented by Mair, as adapted from the translation of James Legge in an early article with the title of "Imperial Confucianism"—a title that suggests how the articles of this virtual "constitution" of Imperial China have been promulgated in the name of a "sage emperor" in such a worshipful manner as to convey the sense that "sage" *(sheng)* is indeed to be understood with all the religious aura of the holy and sacred.

1. Esteem most highly filial piety and brotherly submission, in order to give due importance to the social relations.
2. Behave with generosity towards your kindred, in order to illustrate harmony and benignity.
3. Cultivate peace and concord in your neighborhoods, in order to prevent quarrels and litigations.

4. Recognize the importance of husbandry and the culture of the mulberry tree, in order to ensure a sufficiency of clothing and food.
5. Show that you prize moderation and economy, in order to prevent the lavish waste of your means.
6. Give weight to colleges and schools, in order to make correct the practice of the scholar.
7. Extirpate strange principles, in order to exalt the correct doctrine.
8. Lecture on the laws, in order to warn the ignorant and obstinate.
9. Elucidate propriety and yielding courtesy, in order to make manners and customs good.
10. Labor diligently at your proper callings, in order to stabilize the will of the people.
11. Instruct sons and younger brothers, in order to prevent them from doing what is wrong.
12. Put a stop to false accusations, in order to preserve the honest and good.
13. Warn against sheltering deserters, in order to avoid being involved in their punishment.
14. Fully remit your taxes, in order to avoid being pressed for payment.
15. Unite in hundreds and tithings, in order to put an end to thefts and robbery.
16. Remove enmity and anger, in order to show the importance due to the person and life.[16]

Mair's main interest in the Edict is how, and in what vernacular forms, "the bare bones of Confucian orthodoxy," as he calls them, are purveyed to and elaborated on for a popular audience. We cannot help noting, however, that in the subject matter of the Sixteen Maxims enunciated here there is indeed a heavy emphasis, especially in the later articles, on matters more of concern to a central authority and its bureaucracy than to a local community—matters pertaining to law as administered by magistrates and prefects, the suppression of heterodoxy, the punishment of deserters, the payment of taxes, etc.—which are further detailed in successive elaborations for popular consumption.[17]

Likewise to be noted in Mair's discussion is how the term *xiangyue* is regularly translated as "village lectures," following the conventional rendering by other observers of Qing practice in this regard.[18] The idea of any consensual compact or covenant, as suggested by the original Chinese term *"yue"*—something voluntarily subscribed to or pledged by the members of a community—is nowhere in evidence; in fact the question does not even occur as to whether any kind of consent might be involved, so pervasive is the assumption that what matters is only how well one's subjects may understand and obey the imperial dictate.

The ritual accompaniments to the lectures all contributed to the aura of religious veneration for the ruler and the *Sacred Edict*. An altar was erected as the centerpiece of the affair on which the Emperor's name and the *Sacred Edict* (or expanded versions of it) were set,[19] while incense perfumed the site, candles and flowers decorated it, cantors sang, and the audience were expected to bow and kow-tow at liturgically appropriate moments.[20]

It is not surprising then, when we look at the original Chinese text for one of the most earnest and fulsomely religious prescriptions for the "village lectures" on the *Sacred Edict*, that of Li Laizhang (1654–1721), to find that in the title of his essay on the subject the term for "lecture," *jiangyi*, is replaced by *xuanjiangyi*, in which the last character, a close approximation in both sound and graph to the original *yi*, clearly connotes "rite" or "ceremony" rather than lecture.[21]

The preface to an 1865 vernacular rendering of the *Sacred Edict* eloquently expresses the attitude of veneration expected in the presence of this holy writ handed down from the Imperial Ancestors:

Our Sacred Ancestor, the benevolent Emperor [Kangxi], himself having been given great authority by Heaven, was disposed to display his sympathy for the benighted. He expressly promulgated the *Sacred Edict*, composed of sixteen items, to constitute forever a method of indoctrination. Our Epochal Progenitor, the Exemplary Emperor [Yongzheng], in turn, composed the *Amplified Instructions* in ten thousand words. He also instituted study halls and lectures on the first and fifteenth of each month.

The Plans of the Sages are far-reaching and bright as the sun and the moon. Now the Son of Heaven, at a moment when the empire's fate turns, brings about restoration by diligently seeking order. The Silken Words of the Emperor repeatedly disseminate clear explanations as he lectures on the essentials of the old statutes. Truly this is an important way to transform the people and to reform customs.[22]

One notices here the tone of benign paternalism with which the Emperor bestows his sympathy on the "benighted" people. In strong contrast to the earlier idealistic Neo-Confucian expression of a desire to bring out all of the natural goodness in humankind, there is a crescendo of references in the literature on the "village lectures" to the ignorance and waywardness of the common people, who are repeatedly described as "stupid," "doltish," "idiotic," "slow-witted," "dullards," "imbeciles," and so forth.[23]

Such a low estimation of the popular mentality went hand-in-hand with a condescension on the part of the officials performing in these ceremonies, who professed to take seriously their own paternalistic responsibilities as "shepherds" or "pastors" of the people,[24] even when they may have been relatively perfunctory in discharging their duty.[25] All of this contributes to the sense that the *xiangyue*, understood as "village lectures," were no more than "a method of popular indoctrination," and Mair has no difficulty in finding a plethora of quotations to this effect, e.g., ". . . during the Yongzheng period (1723–1735) all the variant forms of intellectual restriction . . . were channeled towards the same end—the enforcement of orthodox ideology." There was a determined attempt to make this orthodoxy the pattern for the political behavior of everyone within the empire, not just the ideological standard for the literati. Numerous official measures relating to the propagation of the maxims of the *Sacred Edict,* including successive refinements of the village lecture system, were an integral part of this ideological enforcement. Chung-li Chang agrees that the purpose of the semimonthly lectures on what he calls the "politico-moral maxims" of the *Sacred Edict* was to "indoctrinate the masses with the official ideology."[26]

To complete this picture of the "village lecture" system, one needs further to recognize that the ultimate result of the process by which a consensual pact became transformed into an instrument of official indoctrination was that it came increasingly to be regarded as a routine bureaucratic function, performed more and more by prefects, magistrates, or their deputies, and less and less by any independent or quasi-autonomous local gentry. No doubt the nominal aim, and sometimes even the sincere intention of the more dedicated Confucians, was that all persons in any kind of authority should take the matter seriously, but there is much evidence that the lectures were regarded as normally the business of the mandarinate, with the local gentry only marginally involved.[27]

From this it is understandable that observers in the nineteenth century and commentators in the twentieth should come to the conclusion that the "village lectures" and the lectures on the *Sacred Edict* at the other levels were viewed more and more as "empty exercises" and "meaningless rituals." Mair himself concludes, "The reading of the *Sacred Edict* here seems to have become a rather routine part of government business" [354], and that "the official reading of the *Sacred Edict* had already fallen into desuetude" by as early as 1832. To the extent that anything came of efforts to popularize a code of public morality, it was through the non-official vernacular forms of popular entertainment—story-telling and quasi-dramatic performances—that arose alongside of the official ceremonies. "There can be no doubt that the diffusion of Confucian ideals was far more efficiently accomplished through this type of grass-roots activity than through the pompous, ritualistic, and often lifeless ceremonies presided over by local officials" [355].

In the end even the vernacular literature produced by scholar-officials to explain the *Sacred Edict* are seen by Mair as not actually intended to be read by commoners but only to be used as manuals or guidebooks for officials who are responsible for imparting the message orally to the general populace, for "propagating a uniform ideology" [351]. Thus he says, "I found no evidence that the vernacular versions of the *Sacred Edict* and the *Amplified Instructions* were read by the common people on their own initiative" [358].

Hence, when Mair concludes that "this is a clear case of the bearers of high culture consciously and willfully trying to mold popular culture" [356], one can well believe it, but still with an important reservation: this characterization applies primarily to the official elite of the Qing on the bureaucratic level. In view of the takeover of the process by the imperial establishment for its own ideological purposes, it remains an open question whether the same applies to all "bearers of high culture," unofficial as well as official, or whether another view of it might be taken concerning those literati marginalized in the process.

That this last reservation and question may still be pertinent is suggested not only by Mair's acknowledgment, made at the outset of his article, that the history of the *Sacred Edict* and the "village lectures" did not begin with the founding fathers of the Qing, but also by certain clues left along the way that the high tradition carried forward by the "bearers of culture" may actually have been more problematic even than is suggested by Mair's account of its Qing incarnation.

One clue is a brief reference by Mair to the origins of the Qing "lectures" in 1652, wherein he says, "*Six Maxims* were promulgated throughout the land." Further he notes, "Following Ming precedent, an imperial directive was issued in 1659 establishing a system of village lectures *(xiangyue)* to elucidate the *Six Maxims* in plain and simple language on the first and fifteenth of each month. It was this system that was carried over subsequently by lectures on the *Sacred Edict* and continued, with varying degrees of vitality, to the end of the Qing dynasty" [349].

As for the reference to *Six Maxims,* there is also an earlier mention of it as an antecedent *Sacred Edict* attributed to the founder of the Ming dynasty, Ming Taizu (r. 1368–1398) and translated by Mair as follows:

> Be filial to your parents
> Be respectful to your elders
> Live in harmony with your neighbors
> Instruct your sons and grandsons
> Be content with your calling
> Do no evil [327]

Though Mair himself does not elaborate on these Ming antecedents, we are alerted to the fact that the *Sacred Edict* and "village lectures" have already had a history of almost 300 years before the Kangxi version was promulgated. It might also have crossed the reader's mind that, even on a surface comparison of the *Six Maxims* and the Sixteen Maxims of the Kangxi emperor, there are significant differences between the two, the most obvious of which is the greater brevity and simplicity of the earlier model. The greater length and complexity of the Kangxi version is largely attributable to a substantial supplementation of these six ethical maxims, originally well adapted to a local community, by precisely the kind of strictures in the Sixteen Maxims that would serve to enhance state power and imperial authority: namely the enforcement of dynastic law, obedience to the state, crime prevention, punishment of deserters, payment of taxes and tithes, banning of heterodoxy, etc. The next question that might logically arise in the reader's mind would have to do with "the system of village lectures *(xiangyue)*" said to have been inherited from the Ming as a vehicle for propagating first the Six and then the Sixteen Maxims—a question all the more likely to occur to one familiar with the earlier meaning and history of the *xiangyue*. Was there anything in the evolution of the *xiangyue* from community compact to imperially mandated "village lectures" that might parallel, and perhaps help to explain, the great transformation in the content of these maxims?

The answer is yes, but for this we must turn back to the early Ming.

When Victor Mair speaks of the *Sacred Edict* as originally promulgated by Ming Taizu, he is correct in identifying the latter as the source of the *Six Maxims* in the form of a *Sacred* (i.e. Imperial) *Edict*. He seems not to have been aware, however, that the language and content of the *Six Maxims* goes back to Zhu Xi, his local proclamations, and the community compact of the Lü Family, where they have a quite different significance from that given them by Ming Taizu, and later by the Kangxi and Yongzheng emperors of the Qing.

The similarity of the wording of the *Six Maxims* to that found in earlier texts of Zhu Xi, and to other texts resuscitated by Zhu (and preserved in Zhu's *Collected Works*), is so striking that even though Taizu himself cites no such earlier authority, but speaks as if for Heaven itself, there can be little doubt that this wording had been provided to him by Neo-Confucian advisors well acquainted with Master Zhu's works. The specific texts are: (1) the Lü family compact (1076) and Zhu's amended version of it; (2) Zhu's Nankang Proclamation of 1179; (3) Guling xiansheng chuanyu wen of Chen Xiang (1017–1090); and (4) Zhu's Proclamation in Zhangzhou of 1190.

First let us consider the last named of these documents, Zhu Xi's "Proclamation of Instructions" addressed to all members of the *baowu* community unit, literati and commoners alike, giving

Zhu's recommendation for the improvement of public morality. It opens with the following:

> Instructions to members of the community concerning matters about which they should encourage and admonish each other:
>
> Be filial and obedient to parents [both father and mother]
> Be respectful to elders
> Live in harmony with your clansmen and relatives
> Be helpful to your neighbors
> Perform your proper duty
> Let each practice his primary occupation
> Let there be no wantonness or stealing, no drinking or gambling, no fighting with or suing one another.[28]

Here the wording is almost identical to the *Six Maxims (Sacred Edict)* of Ming Taizu. The latter formulation has compressed the slightly longer and more detailed version of Zhu Xi, but the meaning is the same. On the other hand we note that Zhu's exhortations are addressed to members of the community who are to "encourage and admonish" each other in a spirit of mutuality and cooperation.

Now let us look at the item that immediately precedes the above in Zhu's *Collected Works:* "Placard of Master Guling's Instructions [to the Community]." This is a document Zhu publicized as part of his moral uplift campaign, which Zhu typically promoted by citing some recent local precedent and not just the classic books of rites. "Master Guling" is Chen Xiang (1017–1080), like Zhu a native of Fujian and an educator of note, who promulgated this instruction when magistrate of Xianzhu sub-prefecture in Zhejiang.

> The father should be righteous. (He can make his family upright.) The elder brother should have brotherly love. (He should be able to care for his younger brother.) The younger brother should be respectful. (He should be able to respect his elder brother.) The son should be filial. (He should be able to serve

his parents.) Husband and wife should have a sense of obligation to each other. (In dire poverty they should look after each
other, this is to have a sense of obligation; if the husband
abandons his wife and does not look after her, or if the wife
remarries after her husband is dead, this is to lack a sense of
obligation.) There must be a distinction between man and
woman. (A man has a wife and a woman has a husband. The
distinction should not be confounded.) Children should study.
(They should be able to understand ritual decorum, rightness,
integrity, and shame.) The village and hamlet should practice
rituals. (On holidays and festive days greetings and exchanges
of gifts should be based on kindness. In feasting and drinking,
the proper order of old and young should be observed. So
should rituals of sitting and standing, and bowing and rising.)
When dire poverty or hardship is experienced, relatives should
come to the aid of one another. (They should lend money or
rice.) Neighbors and the community should help one another
on occasions of marriage or death. Do not be lax in efforts in
agriculture or sericulture. Do not steal or rob. Do not learn
gambling. Do not indulge in hasty litigation . . .[29]

This instruction is very similar in aim, audience, spirit, and tone
to both Zhu's Zhangzhou proclamation and the Lü family community compact (with which it is roughly contemporaneous). In
particular one should note the emphasis on mutual respect and
cooperation in the conduct of specific human relationships, the
minimizing of external authority and control, and the absence of
any coercive threats. It provides another link between this genre of
instruction and the community compact, helps to explain why
they are grouped together in Zhu's *Collected Writings,* and also
shows how this whole ensemble could be seen as affording precedents for the later "village lectures" of the Ming and Qing.

Most indicative of this close affinity, however, is the note Zhu
Xi attached to the Guling instruction:

In accordance with the above, I now expect that members of
the same community unit *(bao)* should mutually encourage or
restrain each other as follows:

Be filial and obedient to parents; be respectful to elders and superiors; live in harmony with clansmen and relatives; be helpful to your neighbors. Each should perform his proper duty and practice his primary occupation. Let there be no wantonness or stealing, no drinking or gambling, no fighting or suing of one another . . .

One more even earlier proclamation of Zhu Xi was issued in 1179 when he was prefect of Nankang in Jiangsi, where in addition to his celebrated efforts to restore the White Deer Grotto Academy, Zhu also paid attention to public instruction. The language here is not exactly the same as in the preceding excerpts but the general approach and contents are similar. After citing earlier worthy precedents in local tradition and a subsequent lapse, he says:

Now I entreat you, local leaders and elders, to gather at seasonal festivals so as to instruct and admonish the people and to remind them once more at every opportunity, so that everyone of the younger generation will understand and practice filial piety, brotherly respect, loyalty and faithfulness. Within the family, they should know how to serve elders and superiors. They should be nice and generous towards relatives and be kind and helpful towards neighbors. Those who have much should assist those in need. In time of difficulty, they should help one another. It is hoped that thereby the excellence of customs will not fall short of what was seen in the past . . .[30]

I do not need to belabor the similarity in the moral message but only observe that here, as in Master Guling's case and the Lü family compact, the medium is to be a gathering of the community for mutual aid, encouragement, and self-criticism, under the leadership of the literati. In the original Lü compact such a meeting was referred to in the following terms:

Every month there shall be a meeting where a meal is provided. Once every three months there shall be a gathering where wine and a meal is served. The person in charge [each month] shall be responsible for raising the money to cover the expenses. At these meetings the good and bad deeds shall be entered in the registers and rewards and punishments shall be administered. Any difficulty troubling the compact should be remedied after a general discussion *(gongyi).*[31]

Although some evidence exists of attempts to set up community compacts in the late Song and Yuan periods,[32] the concept would not seem well enough established in practice for it to serve directly as an institutional model for the Ming founder to draw upon, had he even wished to do so. More likely it is that his appropriation of ideas for a community moral code drew upon literary sources known to his scholarly advisors through their familiarity with the works of Zhu Xi, namely the texts of the proclamations and compacts just cited. Yet the full significance of this borrowing process lies in more than just the striking similarity of language between the *Six Maxims* and Zhu Xi's precepts for village self-governance. More important is Taizu's adoption of that language while incorporating it into a quite different structure.

As a commoner who had risen from humble beginnings to command a new dynasty, Taizu had a strong sense of himself as a man of the people with, he thought, a better feel for life in the village than most members of the literati possessed. This led him to intensive efforts from on high—perhaps the most intrusive in pre-modern Chinese history—to reach into the villages and organize life on the local level. In part this effort derived from his own feeling of rapport with the common man, yet it arose also from his distrust of the bureaucracy, whose educated talents he depended upon for the administration of so populous an empire, yet whose interests in and interventions into village life he wished to curb.[33] Thus he shared with Zhu Xi a belief in the need to achieve local leadership, but differed from Zhu in his powerful urge to maintain strong overall control, and indeed ruthless personal direction, rather than leave too much to scholar-officials in the state bureaucracy.

As Taizu became ever more distrustful of the bureaucracy and sub-officialdom, and increasingly convinced that corrupt elements on the local level were frustrating his reform efforts, he took to issuing a series of instructions to all his subjects, which were markedly authoritarian, arbitrary, and brusque in manner. These were called "Great Pronouncements" *(dagao)*, the threatening tone of which makes it understandable that they should have come to be viewed as "Great Warnings."[34] This admonitory process culminated in his 1398 "Proclamation of Instructions for the People" *(jiaomin bangwen)* in forty-one articles, covering a wide range of matters concerning local governance. While utilizing the same genre of proclamation as had Zhu Xi and incorporating both ideas and methods from Zhu's community compact, Taizu attempted rigorously to define the functions of the village elders and in particular their responsibility for inculcating his precepts into the general population. Among the heterogeneous, often quixotic, and rather disjointed contents of his Proclamation, the nineteenth article contained the essential elements of what would become the "village lectures," as well as the contents of the so-called *Sacred Edict*. The text reads in part:

> Each community *(xiang)* and village *(li)* shall prepare a bell with a wooden clapper. Old, disabled, or blind people guided by children, shall be selected to walk through the *li* carrying the bell . . . They are to shout loudly and plainly so that everyone can understand, exhorting them to do good and avoid violations of the law. Their message should be: "Be filial and submissive to your parents. Be respectful to your elders and superiors. Live in harmony with your neighbors. Instruct your children and grandchildren. Let each be content with his own occupation. Commit no wrongdoing." This is to be done six times a month. At the time of the autumn harvest the people of the village shall, according to their means, make provision of food, etc. . . .[35]

Here the wording of the first part of the instructions is exactly the same as in Zhu Xi's proclamations, while the latter part consists of adaptations—more general but at the same time more concise formulations—of Zhu's instructions concerning the pursuit of a proper livelihood and the avoidance of wrongdoing. We note too that the *Six Maxims* are preceded by exhortations to encourage good deeds and avoid bad deeds, in the same manner as the mutual encouragement and admonition to be practiced in the community compact (yet again without reference by Taizu to such a compact or any deference to its voluntaristic character).

One other item among the forty-one articles in this proclamation is deserving of note. It is article thirty-two, which recalls the previous existence of community schools *(shexue)* set up earlier in Taizu's reign (1375) to provide moral instruction for the young, following, as we have seen in chapter 4, a similar practice in the Yuan period (urged on Khubilai by his Neo-Confucian educational advisor, Xu Heng, and enacted in 1270).[36]

Taizu's earlier policy to institute universal education through a system of community schools had been hailed by his Neo-Confucian adviser Song Lian (1310–1381) at the time of its adoption in 1375 as an epochal achievement.[37] Although it is not clear to what extent the earlier system was meant to be compulsory and full time for all, the new policy in article thirty-two sanctioned a differentiation between part-time students (largely full-time agriculturalists in the farming season) and those with the means and leisure for full-time study—a throwback to the traditional dichotomy of educated elite and minimally educated "peasants," but probably a concession already implied in Zhang Wenqian's "community schooling," which emphasized popular moral instruction under the Ministry of Agricultural Households (Revenue) rather than the study of classical texts as preparation for civil service examinations, under the Ministry of Rites.[38] Further, Taizu's article thirty-two signified, as a corollary to the above, that in the absence of community schools or any other official school system below the district or county level,[39] public instruction in the villages was to be left largely to the propagation of Taizu's six instructions through the means specified in article nineteen.

Finally, since Taizu linked this system of public indoctrination to the *lijia* system of revenue-raising and local control, in preference to maintaining community schools or establishing (or reestablishing?) a system of community compacts, it substituted for the voluntary and cooperative organization of Zhu Xi's relatively autonomous and self-governing compacts a system run by village elders and headmen (tax-captains) responsible to the state administration.[40] Indeed this outcome was virtually assured when Taizu charged the Ministry of Agricultural Households (or Revenue) to implement the Proclamation for Public Instruction with the following admonition: "After this order is published, any official or sub-official who dares to disobey it will be punished with the utmost penalty, and as for commoners *(minren)* who disobey, they will be exiled to the frontiers with their entire families . . ."[41]

Despite this heavy emphasis in Taizu's edict on obedience to the dictates of the ruler, a striking incongruity appears in the absence, among the public or social virtues so stressed in the Six Instructions or *Sacred Edict,* of any reference to the virtue of *zhong,* loyalty to the sovereign. Japanese scholars who have studied the matter as an aspect of both popular customs and local government in Ming China take this absence as confirming the surviving influence of Zhu Xi on this particular genre, even without any direct attribution to him, inasmuch as he provided the kernel and essential spirit of the Six Instructions.[42] For in Zhu Xi's proclamations, addressed to local populations, he had often stressed filial piety as the root of all virtue and relegated loyalty to the ruler, as a derivative virtue, to secondary status.[43] Indeed this view was one Zhu Xi consistently upheld, whether in local proclamations or even in lectures or precepts addressed to elite audiences at private academies, as for instance in his "Stated Precepts of the White Deer Grotto Academy," wherein the ruler–minister relation—assigned second place after the parent–child relation—is defined not in terms of a bond of personal loyalty and obedience, but [following Mencius] in terms of a mutual acceptance of "rightness" *(yi)* as the guiding principle of their relationship.[44]

The pertinence of all this to local uplift and instruction is that Zhu Xi considered filial piety to be a value and virtue common to all human beings, regardless of social position, class, or political status, whereas rightness had strong contextual, particularistic connotations. Filial piety could thus serve as the ground for a unified political culture rooted in the cooperative life of the family, clan, and village community[45]—an attitude Taizu could share to some degree, even though he promulgated it from on high with all the fierce authority he could command, rather than leave it, as Zhu Xi did, to gentry-led exhortations to villagers at the grassroots level.

Since the *Six Maxims* and the procedures for reading and explaining them in Taizu's Proclamation for Public Instruction had been educational adjuncts to the *lijia* system of village administration, within a century or so after their promulgation, as economic and social changes undermined the workings of the *lijia* system,[46] the conduct of village lectures was left without firm administrative moorings. At this historical juncture, members of the educated elite, whether as scholars or officials, turned in the late fifteenth and early sixteenth centuries to the original framework of the community compact as known through Zhu Xi's version to fill part of the vacuum left by the disintegration of the *lijia* and weakening of the village elder systems. How general this trend became, or how much it was due to local initiative as compared to central direction, remains unclear, yet by the Jiajing period (1522–1566) many examples can be found of community compacts being brought into existence, often in combination with the conduct of the village lectures and reading of the *Six Maxims* or *Sacred Edict*, but also alongside other local institutions Zhu Xi had promoted such as community schools, charitable granaries, *baojia* collective security units and Zhu Xi's Family Rituals.[47] From this concatenation of events, ideas, and institutions we may deduce the influence of Zhu Xi's ideas on successive generations of Ming scholar-officials educated according to the Neo-Confucian curriculum in both official schools and local academies. Moreover, the simultaneous appearance of similar institutions in sixteenth-century Korea, without any preexisting model to follow except what was set forth in Zhu Xi's works, strongly suggests the influence of ideas drawn from a Neo-Confucian intellectual tradition.

In this process there is variation enough in individual cases to suggest that the actual practices were being adapted to local circumstances and exigencies of the moment, with scholars and officials responding according to their own predilections and personal commitments. Nevertheless, in general we may identify the following as significant developments in the sixteenth and seventeenth centuries:

1. There is a wide enough spread and a sufficiently homogeneous content in this movement that a fairly common pattern shows up based on a synthesis of article nineteen in Taizu's Proclamation and Zhu Xi's version of the Lü family community compact.

2. In this process the village lectures on the *Sacred Edict* became fused with the practice of the community compact—a natural enough coalescence, since the moral content of the *Six Maxims* not only came from the same original source as the compact form itself, but now also carried with it the sacred aura of Taizu's imperial authority and dynastic precedent. At first the public lectures were often accompanied by a reading of both the Lü-shih compact text and the *Six Maxims*, but in time the briefer and more concise form of the latter overtook the former.[48] This fusion of the community compact, village lectures, and *Sacred Edict* led to

the popular characterization of the practice by the end of the Ming as *jiangyue,* whereby the nearly homophonous word for lecture *(jiang)* was substituted for "community" *(xiang).*[49] This implied a consequent lessening of emphasis on communitarian participation and mutual aid, and an increasing stress on the didactic aspect of the local ritual—hence the understanding of both *xiangyue* and *jiangyue* as "village lecture" rather than as anything resembling Zhu's original community compact. With this linkage we can now understand how the generic term for community compact, *xiangyue* would have come to be understood by Chinese scholars and foreign observers alike, from the later seventeenth century onwards, as "village lectures."[50]

3. In the course of this routinizing of the practice, however, many conscientious scholar-officials, recollecting the original intent and scope of the community compact conceived by Zhu Xi, attempted to reinstate it and reinvigorate the practice of the compact as a means of dealing more effectively with local crises or special needs. Among the leading scholars who did so were Luo Qinshun (1465–1547), Wang Yangming (1472–1529), Wang Tingxiang (1474–1554), Lo Rufang (1515–1588), Hu Zhi (1517–1585), Lü Kun (1536–1618), Gao Panlong (1562–1626), Liu Zongzhou (1578–1645), and, in the early Qing, Lu Shiyi (1611–1672) and Chen Hongmou (1696–1771).[51]

The most celebrated example of these scholarly adaptations of the community compact is Wang Yangming's. It is also illustrative of the "liberal" uses of the compact by someone appreciative of Zhu Xi's intentions for it as a voluntaristic program for rural reform and moral uplift, based on an appeal to the essential goodness of human nature—a cardinal principle of both Zhu's and Wang's philosophies. Wang had just pacified a local rebellion in Jiangsi, and sought in this proclamation of 1520 to convert a restive population to the acceptance of civil order as "new citizens" *(xinmin)* of a reformed community. Though quite similar in general form to Zhu Xi's version, and inspired by the same intense moral idealism, Wang's compact is extraordinarily detailed in its provisions for all of the members to participate in it as a group, and take responsibility for the recognition and encouragement of those who perform good deeds, as well as the reproving and reform of those who violate community norms. Expressed throughout the document is a deep belief in the power of moral suasion, the ability of the community to agree readily on the norms of proper conduct, and thus the possibility of renewing the common life by consensual means.

A representative passage in Wang's text follows the reproof of both the authorities and the people for their past failings in not "putting inducement and encouragement into practice," or not making "sufficient arrangements for cooperation and coordination."

> The responsibility for all this should be shared by us government officials and all of you, old and young.
>
> Alas! Nothing can be done to change what has already gone by, but something can still be done in the future. Therefore a community compact is now specially prepared to unite and harmonize all of you. From now on, all of you who enter into this compact should be filial to your parents and respectful to your elders, teach your children, live in harmony with your fellow villagers, help one another when there is death in the family and assist one another in times of difficulty, encourage one another to do good and warn one another not to do evil, stop litigations and rivalry, cultivate faithfulness and promote harmony, and be sure to be good citizens so that together you may establish the custom of humanity and kindness . . . All of you, both old and young, do not remember the former evil deeds of the new citizens and ignore their good deeds. As long as they have a single thought to do good, they are already good people. Do not be proud that you are good citizens and neglect to cultivate your personal life. As long as you have a single thought to do evil, you are already evil people. Whether people are good or evil depends on a single instant of thought. You should think over my words carefully. Don't forget . . .[52]

Although much has been made by later scholars of the philosophical differences between Zhu Xi and Wang Yangming, and
here and there one can detect some differences in emphasis (for
instance, Wang's declaration that "Whether people are good or
evil depends on a single instant of thought" [*yinian*]),[53] for the
most part the spirit, form, and language of the discourse on
community compacts is remarkably similar among thinkers
across the philosophical spectrum.

Heirs to the Neo-Confucian tradition in Yi dynasty Korea,
though in somewhat different circumstances, express themselves
in much the same fashion. I shall refrain from undue repetition
of the point by quoting writings on this subject of the great
Neo-Confucian scholars, Yi Hwang (T'oegye) (1501–1570) and Yi
I (Yulgok) (1536–1584), but I believe any reader who consults
the discussion of the matter by Sakai Tadao[54] will recognize that
the Korean proponents of the community compact are exponents
of a distinct Neo-Confucian tradition, expressed in terms of the
same textual discourse and generic practices, while in the process
also making their own original adaptations to local and temporal
circumstances.

From the detailed studies of late Ming community compacts
made by Joseph McDermott, it is clear that the original impetus
for the implementation of such compacts in the Ming came from
individual Neo-Confucian scholar-officials such as those men-
tioned above, whose local initiatives, inspired by Zhu Xi's adaptation of the Lü family compact, bore the distinctive marks of his
teaching, including his primary emphasis on filial piety and community cooperation, rather than loyalty to the ruler.[55] After the
breakdown of the *lijia* system, such initiatives were first taken as
early as 1438 on the local level and only belatedly given endorse-
ment in 1529 by a court that had until then paid little attention
to such things.[56] The reigning emperor of the Jiajing period
(1522–1566), preoccupied with his personal pursuit of Daoist
cults and rituals, took little interest in reform proposals from his

Confucian officials. In the late sixteenth century, however, an increasing sense of political crisis and the government's feeling of a need to enlist and exploit local organizations as a means of achieving greater control and political stability led to greater state involvement. Unfortunately this interest tended to be counterproductive rather than a source of revitalization. It was an intervention from above that was more apt to be stultifying than invigorating—a routinizing of a ritual that brought more and more official posturing and rhetoric.[57] This then set the stage for the more authoritarian, bureaucratized *xiangyue* known in the Qing as the "village lectures" and *Sacred Edict.*

A major long-term interest among twentieth-century Japanese scholars in Chinese studies has been in questions of local autonomy, self-government, and cooperative organization on the local level, assuming (as Western scholars have done from time to time) that rural China or village China was the "real China." In one such study dealing with education in the village, Suzuki Kenichi,[58] extending the pioneering work of Sakai Tadao, has come to a conclusion concerning the history of the community compact that is relevant to our inquiry here.

Given the decline of the *lijia* system of rural organization, Suzuki believes that the Ming dynasty persisted in, and even redoubled, its efforts to promote the "village lectures" and *Six Maxims* as a means of registering the supremacy and centrality of dynastic authority in the popular consciousness, even when that authority was exercised ostensibly on behalf of a rather homespun domestic morality in the "village lectures." In this respect the state cared less about the decline of relatively autonomous local organizations, such as the *lijia*, than it did about establishing a direct link in people's minds between the ruler and his subjects. Here his "subjects" are to be understood as individualized, and in a sense "privatized"—to be dealt with in accordance with the paradigm of the *Great Learning*, in which the self and family were the basis of the social order on the local level, but there was little or no public infrastructure mediating between that level and the state (as we have noted above).

In effect, if we may extend Suzuki's observations, the ruler and his bureaucracy would represent the public interest, and the family clan or lineage would represent a private sphere—but one, however autonomous in its own domestic or local affairs, still politically fragmented vis-à-vis the state. Like all generalizations, this is oversimplified, subject to temporal and local qualification, but it corresponds to a situation in which education on the local level became increasingly the business of the family, clan, or lineage, while "public" schooling served the state's purposes of bureaucratic recruitment.

If this was the "real China" on the local level, I believe it helps to explain why late nineteenth- and early twentieth-century reformers in China saw it as weakened by the split between private loyalties ("excessive individualism," as they called it) and a dynastic state that could not effectively command or mobilize people's loyalties. The flaw, as they saw it, consisted in the lack of a larger community to serve as a bridge between the self-regulation of the family below and the law and order of the state above. Hence, when China encountered the power and mobility of the West in the nineteenth century, it found the "peasant"/farmer standing stock still, his feet stuck politically in the mud of the paddy-field, while the Emperor sat above on his throne, resplendent in imperial robes, but without any civil underclothing beneath the facade of bureaucratic rule.

Conclusion

From this brief survey of the successive stages in the life of the community compact, we can conclude, I believe, that it survived for more than half a millennium of pre-modern East Asian history both as an agency of the state reaching in to the local village, and as a liberal Neo-Confucian tradition, embodying both ideas and institutions and their actual practice in variant forms. By "liberal" I mean that as a form of scholarly advocacy, and in some actual local cases, it upheld the principles of voluntarism, local autonomy, consensual and cooperative arrangements for the improvement of village life, the minimizing of autocratic and bureaucratic interference on the local level, and the sustaining of responsible leadership on the basis of shared values rooted in the daily life of the common people. It can also be termed a "tradition" in the sense that it was transmitted as a literate discourse through texts that sustained certain ideals and models even when their institutionalization fell well short of fulfilling the idealists' aspirations. On the other hand, in the actual implementation of these values and practices, one could often see them misappropriated in ways characteristic of a more authoritarian, if not indeed autocratic, tradition—a tradition closely, and persistently over time, identified with imperial rule and a well-entrenched bureaucratic state.

If we are dealing with what may be called two parallel traditions so understood, we recognize that members of the Confucian educated class, as a leadership elite, often were caught up in both traditions at once, to greater or lesser degree. Hence the actualities of their life situations were marked by poignant ambiguities, caught between opposing poles and experiencing a strong tension between the two—a tension endured and lived out by an amphibious Confucian elite, with one foot in the soil of rural China and the other in the halls of power.

For all this ambiguity, however, the important point to be registered is that the genuine communitarian tradition in China, as represented by leading Confucian thinkers, strove to maximize voluntary cooperation versus the state's persistent tendency to appropriate community organizations for its own authoritarian purposes. Communitarianism cannot be claimed for the state, as it is today, in the name of Confucianism; indeed, the Confucian record belies any such claim at all on the part of the Chinese state.

Moreover, mixed though the record may be between the actual involvement in government of officials less committed to Confucian ideals than to their own career advancement, and, on the other side, the major thinkers and teachers who kept the communitarian tradition alive, the latter did succeed in sustaining a continuing discourse and debate from age to age, and from China to the rest of East Asia. The importance of the latter, despite the lack of success in realizing these ideals, should not be minimized. They have continued as an important traditional resource for reformers in the twentieth century.

6

Chinese Constitutionalism and Civil Society

In the West the discussion of human rights has usually been couched in legal terms, and there has been a strong tendency to rely on the law for the defense of such rights. The Confucian tradition, as we have seen earlier, has had little faith in law, and instead has emphasized the practice of civility and mutual respect through the observance of "rites," understood as forms of civil decorum that embody sentiments of humane concern and respect for others. These were defined relationally and contextually as norms appropriate in given circumstances, some constant in human affairs and others variable. In the two cases, China (indeed all of Confucian East Asia) and the West, there have been varying degrees of reliance on both laws and consensual norms of social behavior, but the Confucian tradition has been especially marked by its emphasis on "rites" as a means of educating people to voluntary observance of the norms of conduct in socially differentiated situations. Thus in traditional China there has been a place for both laws and rites, but Confucians have given priority to the latter as dealing more profoundly and incisively with basic human motivations through ritual education. Most often Confucian communitarian projects have been conceived as rites, not as laws or systems.

This chapter continues the discussion of laws and rites, treating not only their strengths but their weaknesses as vehicles in China for the expression of human respect, care, and concern for others. From what we have already observed, however, the fate of Confucian communitarianism conceived as consensual rituals fell victim to the superior power of the state system. Thus, regardless of the priority given to ritual or the tradition of Confucian communitarianism, historically the strength of central administration dominated the scene at this crucial level, with dynastic institutions and laws prevailing over Confucian social prescriptions. One could not then expect much improvement on the level of the community, or the emergence of something like a civil society, without addressing the problem of the state.

In taking up this question, I focus here on laws, and especially on constitutional law, which in the West has been seen as the basic framework for upholding human rights, but in China has played a more problematic role, inasmuch as Chinese experience with law reflects a continuing tension between state power above and local society below. Much can be learned from the common ground found here with human rights concepts in the West, as well as from the significant differences in the historical experience of the Chinese. It goes without saying that to examine the Western experience from a Confucian perspective would yield a similar benefit, though this happens not to be the point of the present inquiry.

Here I shall first discuss attitudes towards law held by the Confucians and the principal alternative view held by the so-called Legalists; next, the dynastic codes of the Tang and Ming, as exemplifying the basic law of the imperial dynasties; then critiques of dynastic law offered by prominent Neo-Confucians in the twelfth and seventeenth centuries; and finally some speculations as to the possible relevance of these earlier views to the prospects for constitutionalism and human rights in contemporary China.

As we saw earlier, in recent human rights debates there has been a disposition in some Asian quarters to deprecate Western human rights concepts as too individualistic, and to favor instead an "Asian" view purportedly more communitarian in its concerns. Yet, on closer examination, recent proponents of the "communitarian" view most often turn out to mean by this something more like "statist," i.e., they defend the right of the state to act on behalf of the people as a whole, often at the expense of the individual. What is missing in the argument is any consideration of the community as a form of infrastructure that might mediate between individuals and the state, and perform the function of a civil society in protecting the interests of either the individual or people in groups (rather than en masse). Yet, as we have observed, some of the greatest Confucian thinkers were deeply concerned with precisely this matter, and gave serious attention to the problem of the community, only to find their efforts vitiated by the interventions of an autocratic state, represented by laws and systems prejudicial to the consensual, voluntaristic character of the Confucian rites.

At this point, then, it is appropriate to consider how the Chinese formulation of basic law—the rough counterpart of constitutionalism in the West—affects our understanding of the relationship between state, community, and individual, and of the systemic factors associated with Chinese dynastic law that conditioned the actual implementation of Confucian ritual ideals.

In chapter 3 we saw how early Confucians like Mencius and Xunzi conceived *fa* not as Legalist "law" but as model institutions of the sage-kings, exemplary for civilized society if not exactly for "civil society" as understood in the modern West. Subsequently this conception became incorporated in the expression *xianfa* (lit. "exemplary models") to represent the idea of a constitution in modern East Asian parlance, though in its original form *xianfa* was conceived more as the power (charisma) of personal example than as legal institutions backed by the power of the state. From the time of the classical Confucians to the present, however, two major developments affected the conception of fundamental law in the dominant Confucian tradition. One was the rise of the imperial dynastic system, with laws serving its own purposes, not arrived at by any consensual means; the other was the Neo-Confucian criticism of dynastic law in that form. In the dialectical process between them, something like a proto-constitutionalism emerged among Confucian scholars.

Dynastic law in its institutionalized form emerged from the centralized administrative structures of the Qin dynasty in the third century BCE. Initially these were strongly influenced by the Legalist school of thought, which deliberately repudiated Confucian family-centered morality and stressed instead the universality of law and its impartial (impersonal) administration. This stood in contrast to the particularism and forms of interpersonal respect so stressed by the Confucians, whose humanist universalism was always to be adapted to local circumstances and relational contexts. Its own universalistic aspect is what renders the Legalist conception most akin to modern conceptions of constitutionalism, but no less relevant for our purposes is its stress on systems, especially in the form of systematic rational management and total control of human affairs by the state. Thus law as developed by the Legalists was perceived as an instrument of state power, imposed on the people for their own good but not ratified by any consensual process. Law and the state were absolute in their authority. There was no sense of an alternative source or channel of authority or of a need for countervailing powers—checks and balances—such as modern constitutionalism has most often attempted to provide.

Dynastic Law

Although the Qin dynasty itself proved short-lived, the memory of its totalitarian controls and reliance on harsh punishments endured in traditional historiography. At the same time many of its administrative structures were preserved by the Han dynasty, which set the pattern for later imperial regimes. Characteristic of this pattern were the following:

1. A rejection of Legalist totalitarianism, its punitive, deterrent methods, and its assertion of state power for its own sake. Along with this, however, came a reaffirmation of state authority in the guise of a benevolent paternalism, based on a Confucian conception of true rulership as responding to people's needs, expressed especially by Dong Zhongshu.

2. Continuance of the essential Legalist apparatus for central administration, while at least nominally elevating Confucian rites to a higher place than penal law in the formal structures of the empire. This acknowledged the inherent limitations of law in the form of centralized controls, and allowed greater scope in the hinterland for local tradition and especially clan- and family-centered rituals. In other words, the dynastic pattern implied a modus vivendi or coexistence between a rationalized, central bureaucracy overall, and a looser, more autonomous, customary practice on the local level, where the Confucian ethos was thought generally to prevail. To this extent both in theory and practice the Han system acknowledged necessary limits on the exercise of state power, while still asserting the supremacy of the ruler's authority by virtue of his role in keeping the peace and fulfilling his paternalistic responsibility to provide for the guidance and welfare of the people.

3. In place of a Legalist rationale for basic law, the dynastic constitution or ultimate authority was vested in the exemplary enactments of the founder of the dynasty, seen as legal precedents for his heirs, who were bound by filial obligation to perpetuate the regime and its founding institutions, to which they had succeeded. Inheritance of power and authority brought corresponding responsibilities. Thus the Confucian virtue of filial piety was invoked on behalf of dynastic laws conceived, not as a systematic and coherent legal structure, but as exemplary models of superior virtue (and thus of charismatic power) on the part of the founding father(s).

Insofar as superior virtue was identified with a Heaven-ordained moral law and rulers were answerable to this higher "law," it constituted a moral constraint on the exercise of power. For practical purposes, however, the effectiveness of this constraint upon the Son of Heaven depended on the readiness of his ministers, on whose assistance the ruler clearly depended for carrying out his dictates, to articulate these sentiments at the imperial court and make them prevail. There was no other "constituted" court to which recourse might be had in cases of dispute. Failing in this, Confucian ministers were obliged to resign and leave court, according to Mencius, rather than become associated with actions and policies that were not "right" *(yi)*. It was then up to members of the ruling house, seeing him abandoned by his ministers, to depose the ruler. Otherwise if conditions deteriorated seriously, revolt of the people was the final court of appeal, with the people speaking for Heaven, as the saying went: "Heaven speaks as the people speak." Still, this is not constitutionalism, which in any language must imply orderly process (as it did for Mencius himself), not a resort to violence.

Traditionally in East Asia the most widely admired formulation of dynastic law was found in the Great Tang Code. This too embodies the same synthesis as seen in the Han, of regulations designed to assert and preserve the power of the dynastic state along with prescriptions according a large role to customary, and especially family, ritual on the local level. There was, however, nothing consensual or contractual about this basic law. It was an instrument of state power that also recognized certain inherent limits in the power to enforce it over a widely dispersed, but densely populated, realm.

As a rational, systematic formulation for the uses of that power, the Tang Code was widely emulated in seventh-, eighth-, and ninth-century East Asia—in Korea, Japan, and Vietnam—as a model of advanced civilization for societies in the process of state building. Moreover, as a document that sought to recapitulate time-honored legal practices, with organic links to past human experience, the Tang Code showed itself to possess a remarkable durability, its basic provisions reappearing again and again in later dynastic formulations, which themselves claimed a legitimacy deriving from strong continuity with the past.

It should be borne in mind also that though the Tang Code itself tends to emphasize the penal aspects, there was a great deal of other legislation in the Tang that would be better characterized as administrative law, and this too tended to become a model for those other states that emulated this great dynasty as the center of world civilization.

In the development of Chinese dynastic law, the next major codification to have wide influence was that of the founder of the Ming dynasty, Zhu Yuanzhang or officially Ming Taizu, in the late fourteenth century. In its essential character this Ming "constitution" did not differ greatly from the Tang Code, but its spirit and tone reflected the personality of the founder, whose rise to power (and later enactments) manifested the indomitable will of a lowly peasant triumphing over all adversities and adversaries to become the supreme autocrat of a great empire. In the process he laid the foundation for much of the legal and ideological framework for later imperial China. This included the concentration of all legitimate decision-making authority in the hands of the emperor (by abolishing the prime ministership); the imposition of centralized controls over the extended imperial bureaucracy; and the use of one or another form of the merit principle as the proper way to recruit officials.

By 1368, Ming Taizu made himself literate enough to start composing what became a large number of essays, colloquies, commentaries, Confucian-style moral exhortations, and political and social regulations. Through these he defined his own role as both ruler and teacher of China, striving to reach out directly to everyone in the realm, so as to explain to them his own conception of the well-ordered society. Although few of his successors in the Ming could sustain Taizu's comprehensive vision, many of his ideas and enactments nonetheless remained influential through succeeding reigns and into the next dynasty. Though far from representing anything like "constitutionalism" in the modern West, many of Taizu's enactments were accepted as authoritative in the Ming, by his Manchu successors in the succeeding Qing dynasty, by the Korean Yi dynasty, and by rulers in Vietnam.

One of Taizu's most famous enactments was his abolition of the prime ministership after the exposure of an alleged plot by the existing prime minister to usurp the throne. Thenceforth all executive power was concentrated in the emperor, assisted by a secretariat. His system persisted through the late imperial period. He claimed to have the sanction of antiquity, but for its enforcement he relied on his own indomitable will, not the force of tradition: "From now on, when my descendants become emperors, they absolutely shall not establish a prime minister. If there are officials who dare to memorialize requesting such establishment, civil and military officials shall immediately submit accusations. The offender shall be put to death by slicing and his whole family executed."[1]

With such threats and imprecations Ming Taizu confirmed in blood the tradition of ancestral law as a "constitutional order"—in the minimal sense that Taizu's strictures were meant to establish regular processes of government, binding on his successors and thus limiting their individual freedom in the arbitrary exercise of their power. Since in China there existed no separate and independent court to resolve "constitutional" issues, the burden fell on the Emperor and his Confucian advisors to decide things as best they could, or would, in the light of their sense of filial obligation to the founding father. Thus from start to finish the "constitutional order" remained within the orbit of dynastic rule, and while the court could not be wholly unresponsive to popular opinion in arriving at decisions, one could not say that this order was consensual either in its original formulation or in its later practice, there being no infrastructure by which popular sentiment could become informed, articulated, or autonomously structured so as to contribute its own authentic voice to the decision-making process.

Neo-Confucian Critiques of Dynastic Law

Filial piety constituting the root, even if not the highest, virtue in Confucian thought, it could not but loom large in the minds of Confucian ministers and officials serving the Chinese imperial court, who were thereby committed to upholding the best interests of the ruling dynasty. In the Song period, however, Confucian thought underwent a major restructuring in response to pressing challenges—ideological, economic, and social. In dealing with great crises, activist reformers found ancestral precedent alone insufficient to provide for situations unanticipated by the founder, or else, if narrowly and literally interpreted, too cramped for effective policy formulation. It is understandable then that such reformers in the eleventh century, the best known of them Wang Anshi (1021–1086), should ground their reform proposals neither in ancestral law nor the precedents of prestigious earlier dynasties, such as the Han and Tang, but in classical texts bearing the higher authority of great antiquity and the early sage-kings. For this purpose Wang and other reformers found it convenient to invoke the idealized "constitution" of the Zhou dynasty, the so-called *Offices of Zhou (Zhouguan)*, otherwise known as the *Rites of Zhou (Zhouli)*, to express the Confucian preference for rites rather than laws or systems as the basis of the social order. Though purportedly an account of the Zhou government at its founding, the *Rites of Zhou*, assumed into the Confucian canon during the Han dynasty, was probably composed in the late Zhou period as an idealized, prescriptive model, rather than as a straight historical description. While susceptible to varying interpretations (including those cited in chapter 1), the very adaptability of the *Rites of Zhou* lent itself to appropriation by radical reformers as a higher authority that could be invoked in order to bypass ancestral precedent and dynastic law. Viewing the early sage-kings as the true founding fathers of civilization, these reformers were able to relativize dynastic law and establish a higher, more sacred ground in the Confucian classics for a new, overarching constitutional order transcending the temporal limits of dynastic law. In the Song period certainly this contributed to a sense that dynastic law (the precedents of the founder and his successors) was far from untouchable or unalterable.[2]

None of this involved a direct, overt attack on dynastic law. Nevertheless, the finality and absoluteness of ancestral precedent had been questioned. Thus in subsequent discussions of what constituted ultimate authority, no less a thinker and scholarly authority than Zhu Xi (1130–1200), the dominating philosophical figure in late imperial China and himself often critical of Wang Anshi, confirmed the Neo-Confucian position that no historical figure or dynasty could claim fully to embody the Way (and thereby assert absolute authority to speak for it); nor, if there were a conflict between ancestral precedent and the models established by the sage-kings, could the former prevail against the latter. The higher authority of the sages, the Duke of Zhou and Confucius especially, overrode the founding fathers of later dynasties.[3]

One cannot say that this philosophic point of Zhu Xi's became an accepted principle in the politics of the Court, for all of the high respect in which Zhu Xi came to be held. Nevertheless, his political views in other respects served to call into question the laws and systems of the dynastic state, inasmuch as he placed them lower on the scale of political values and priorities. Not that he called for their outright abrogation or non-enforcement, but for him, resort to laws of a punitive variety (as was clearly the case with much of the Tang Code, and would be so later with the Ming) should be a last recourse. The first priority in governance, and the primary model to be set before others, should be one of responsible leadership as manifested through the self-cultivation and self-discipline of the ruler and his surrogates. In other words, law enforcement would be unnecessary if, following the leader's example, everyone practiced self-discipline in accordance with the rites. Hence the widely quoted maxim among the later followers of Zhu Xi throughout East Asia: "self-cultivation (or self-discipline) for the governance of men" *(xiuji chiren).*

Against this background we may appreciate better the contribution of the seventeenth-century Neo-Confucian Huang Zongxi (1610–1695), who comes closest to offering a constitutional program resembling, in some important respects, the constitutional systems of the modern West. The basis for this lies in Huang's masterwork, the *Mingyi daifang lu* (1662), the title of which defies literal translation, but which I render somewhat freely as *Waiting for the Dawn: A Plan for the Prince.*

Huang's main points may be summarized briefly as follows:

1. He sets aside the old Confucian dichotomies of laws versus personal virtue and laws versus rites, stating unequivocally the need for basic law. Without its support, no individual, no matter how virtuous, cultivated, or self-disciplined, can hope to contend with the evils in human society and especially in dynastic rule. As Huang put it, "Should it be said that 'there is only governance by men, not governance by law,' my reply is that only if there is governance by law can there be governance by men. Since unlawful laws fetter men hand and foot, even a man capable of governing cannot overcome inhibiting restraints and suspicions."[4]

2. Here for the first time Huang explicitly rejects the claims of dynastic law, which he calls "unlawful laws"—"unlawful" because they serve the private interests of the imperial family rather than the interest of the people. This debased law is not just to be de-emphasized, but totally invalidated by comparison to the higher Law of the Early Kings as enunciated by Confucius and Mencius.

3. By this new conception of law as higher than the state, and by his subjecting of the ruler to this higher law, Huang attempts to impose a constitutional limitation on the ruler's power (legally defined and structurally incorporated in the organization of government), rather than continuing to put faith in the ruler's capacity for self-restraint, a defect not only of Confucian thinking but of Daoist and Legalist thought as well.

4. Law, as Huang advocates it, is to serve as a countervailing force, strengthening the position of the scholar-official *(shi)*, in his role as public servant, from the arbitrariness of the ruler. In this way Huang drew from the Neo-Confucians' unhappy Ming experience a new lesson concerning the individual's need for law and the importance of law for the curbing of imperial power. Prior to this, in the Song, Yuan, and Ming, Neo-Confucians had put their hope in persuading rulers to perform as sage-kings by listening to the advice of wise mentors and observing the moral constraints of traditional ritual. From this hope sprang their strenuous efforts to elevate and reinforce the position of the Confucian minister.[5] Yet as Huang reviewed the results of this effort over several centuries, he could no longer believe that the individual heroism and dedication of the Noble Person *(junzi)* as minister was sufficient to cope with the inordinate power of the ruler or the latter's indisposition to accept the self-discipline that goes with sage-kingship or the restraints embodied in the rites. Something more would be needed: a supporting infrastructure such as that later identified by Montesquieu in *L'Ésprit des Lois* (1748) with the "corps intermediaries" between state and society at large.

It is not, certainly, that Huang believes any the less in the noble calling of the Confucian scholar-official as exemplified by such heroes as Fang Xiaoru, Hai Rui, and indeed Huang's own father, who had died in a eunuch prison as the price for speaking out against corruption at court. But whatever effect such heroics might have on the moral climate of the age and the court, this lofty political vocation needed support and structural reinforcement at every level. Accordingly, in the recommendations of his plan, Huang calls repeatedly for strengthening the status and identity of the scholar-official class *(shi)* and expanding both their numbers and functions—giving them an increased role in civil government generally, but especially an enhanced status as ministers—with the prime minister, as leader of the *shi,* in an executive position strong enough to balance the power of the emperor.[6]

The institutions Huang recommends would fulfil at least some of the same functions as do the organs of representative government in Western democracies. Especially as embodied in his proposal for a strong prime minister and for ministers who are servants of the people's interests and the common good *(gong),* and who cannot be arbitrarily overruled by the ruler, this constitutional order would have certain resemblances to the present British system of government. Moreover, in the great importance that he attaches to schools, going far beyond their immediate educative functions and setting them up as centers for the expression of public opinion, Huang intends that they should perform much the same purpose as political parties or parliaments.[7] Indeed, considering the whole trend of Chinese political history, it is quite natural that he should think of them in this light. What were called "factions" *(dang)* at the Chinese court represented the nearest thing to the political parties of the West, and, insofar as these factions were alignments based on political principles rather than mere cliques held together by personal loyalties, they tended to become identified with certain schools, as in the late Ming dynasty. Unquestionably, Huang's conception of the high place of schools in the political sphere is a response to the attacks that had been made in the late Ming on precisely this role of the schools as organs of political expression.

A more fundamental reason, perhaps, why schools should seem to Huang the most suitable representatives of public opinion may be found in the traditional structure of Chinese society itself. In the absence of a strong middle class, which in the West has usually provided the basis for an effective party system, it was more natural to turn for this purpose to some institution indispensably bound up with the scholar-official class for whom the state had an inescapable need in its recruitment of officials, the carrying out of bureaucratic functions, etc. Other than this there was no real ground for political parties to stand on, no organized class or group for them to represent. Nor were there, beneath the ruling bureaucracy and its territorial agents, any corporate institutions or voluntary associations with sufficient economic power, social position, and established political rights to make themselves a force to be reckoned with. There was only the mass of common people, for the most part farmers, inarticulate in policy matters and unaccustomed to political action on a wide scale except in the form of violent revolt. In such a situation the schools alone provided some mechanism for the expression of—not public, perhaps, but at least informed—opinion, since schools were indispensable to the training of the ruling class itself. Although, as we have seen in chapter 4, most schools tended to be dominated by the examination culture of late Imperial China, the overt attempts to suppress them and to make them subservient to the ruling power show that schools were considered to be dangerous centers of opposition in a state that placed such a premium on learning. Even in modern times this has continued to be so; for, with the imposition of one-party rule during most of the twentieth century in China, schools and research institutes have remained the most articulate centers of political discussion in mainland China.

It is from this perspective that I would attach significance to Huang's proposals for the strengthening of the educational system and of the educated scholar-official's role in government. As we have seen, successive generations of Neo-Confucians had insisted on the need to expand education as a prerequisite to more informed participation by the people in government. The failure of these efforts (as well as of formal gestures in the direction of a universal school system by Khubilai Khan in the Yuan, and Ming Taizu later) provide a background for this renewed advocacy by Huang Zongxi.

Because Huang is far more pointed than any of his predecessors in asserting, by his special attention to law *(fa)*, the necessary form in which to institutionalize these Confucian values, it seems to me that Huang's plan goes far towards drawing up a systemic order, a kind of Confucian constitution, in a way that no one before him had tried to do. True, it differs in form from most Western constitutions, and is perhaps most distinguishable from the Western type in that, while both are predicated on the implied consent of the governed (on making the people, not the ruler, "masters" in the land, as Huang put it), the contractual element so prominent in Western parliamentary systems (a document ratified by elected representatives, and implemented through electoral processes) is largely absent. In Huang's mythic account of the origin of rulership, he does not speak of the people as coming together and establishing a ruling order where before there was none. Instead, he pictures a state of affairs in which individuals were going about their own business, taking care of themselves, but when a sage-king stood forth and showed, by his own self-sacrificing efforts, how a better order of things could be managed, civilization came into being. Thereafter it was a question of whether other high-minded Noble Men could be persuaded to emulate this self-denying role, not whether any contractual agreement, ratified by the people and binding on both parties, would be arrived at.

Thus we may call Huang's plan a Confucian constitutionalism—"Confucian" insofar as it depends on the personal vocation of the Noble Man and the esprit de corps of the *shi*. It is nonetheless a constitution in the systemic sense insofar as Huang will no longer rely simply on the good intentions and exemplary character of the ruler, but insists on institutionalized limits to the exercise of the ruler's power.

Thus he makes the proposal—shocking to the more conventionally-minded—that the Emperor and his ministers should sit periodically as students at the Imperial College and listen while the libationer (i.e. rector or chancellor) conducted a discussion of current issues among the scholars in attendance.[8] Both symbolically and practically he asserted the higher intellectual and moral authority of the scholarly community in a way that dramatically challenged imperial claims to ultimate authority. And further, he sought to generalize this deference to "public opinion" (*gonglun* or *gongyi*) as a pattern to be followed on all levels of education and administration.

Plainly my use of the term "public opinion" cannot refer to the people or popular opinion as a whole, inasmuch as the great mass of the populace, unschooled and largely illiterate, would have been unable to participate significantly in the process of generating and expressing opinion or forming any general consensus, there being few media of communication or discussion available outside of the literati. "Public" (*gong*) refers to opinion generated both within the government and autonomously outside the state apparatus, and to discussion that addresses issues of concern to "all-under-Heaven," i.e. issues affecting society as a whole and not the interests of the state or dynasty alone.

Literati and scholar-officials called such discussion *jiangxue*, literally "the discussion of learning" or "intellectual discussion." It was mainly carried on in the Ming local academies, or *shuyuan*, literally "centers of book-learning" or "libraries," considered "private" schools to the extent that support for them had to come from among local literati without whose collegial solidarity it would be impossible to carry on open discussion.[9] Thus it was in a scholarly and academic—that is, mostly elite—setting that this kind of public forum was conducted, by a class who thought of themselves as dedicated to public service. It was to this experience that Huang referred when he spoke of establishing this "public" function in a system of government schools, with the libationer leading a discussion *(jiangxue)* open to any and all issues.[10] Huang's aim to create a public space for the airing of important matters is made unambiguously clear when he asserts, in the opening lines of his essay on Schools, that the Son-of-Heaven in ancient times did not try to decide "right and wrong" for himself but left this to be publicly aired and decided by the schools *(gong qi shifei yu xuexiao)*.

The fact that he uses the language of the Neo-Confucian academy, "the discussion of learning" *(jiangxue)* and "public discussion" *(gongyi)*, to describe the essential function to be carried on in this public space, rather than the language of teaching, instructing, or indoctrinating, tells us that he is drawing on the one tradition and institution available as a working example, the Confucian academy, trying to incorporate its characteristic activity in a legally established and protected constitutional body. Moreover, he is broadening its application—its public dimension—by stipulating that the scholar *(ru)* chosen to head the prefectural and district schools may be anyone with the requisite personal qualifications, even a commoner, and need not be someone accredited through the civil service exams, but could be quite unconnected to the state.

Huang defended the intellectual autonomy of the "local" academies themselves, but here he aims to establish this open discussion as a public function both in state schools and at court (where he specifies that the discussion of state matters should be thoroughly aired by the prime minister and his ministers, who are to be qualified scholar-officials). This has much to say about his constitutional intentions. His scholarly forum was to be a well-defined, state-supported, fully accredited, and legal function of a duly constituted order, and yet as independent as possible in a society that lacked a middle class, popular press, church, legal profession or other supporting infrastructure independent of the state. At the same time it must be noted that by open discussion of public questions, Huang did not mean complete freedom of expression in all matters. As a Confucian he believed the upholding of strict moral standards was necessary to the social and political order; thus he was prepared to ban, on the local level, forms of moral impropriety and social corruption.[11]

In the foregoing all-too-brief summary I have given special attention to the views of Huang Zongxi because, in my estimation, they sum up the long experience of the Confucians with dynastic rule and especially the best reflections of Neo-Confucian thinkers in the pre-modern period. I would not claim that Huang's ideas constitute a "tradition" in themselves, because subversive as they clearly were of the dynastic system, they could only be circulated and shared discreetly among a limited number of the Confucian educated elite in the late seventeenth century. Admittedly they represent no sustained political movement. Nevertheless Huang was recognized as a leading scholar of his day, and what he had to say resonated with other leading scholars like Gu Yanwu, Lü Liuliang and Wang Fuzhih. As Lynn Struve, a prime modern authority on the intellectual history of the late seventeenth century, has said of him: "Huang was widely regarded as one of the most learned men of the age; his published views in any area of inquiry would not have lacked readers."[12] Moreover, in the late nineteenth century, when the Western and Japanese impact on China was powerful enough to shake the foundations of Manchu dynastic rule, scholarly reformers as well as revolutionary leaders like Sun Yat-sen, both those influenced by the West and those of a more traditional Confucian persuasion, quickly turned to Huang's work as a way of linking up Western constitutionalism with the Chinese historical experience.

On still other intellectual grounds, Huang's ideas commanded respect because anyone in East Asia familiar with the Confucian scholarly tradition would recognize the superior authority of

Huang Zongxi as an eminent intellectual historian, classicist, literary critic, and so on. By no means could he be belittled as a minor figure with idiosyncratic views that just happened to co-incide with new trends from the West. True, some recent scholars in the West have tended to dismiss such purported resemblances between Western thought and Chinese tradition as contrived and forced, on the ground that the two were not congruent in all respects. Such critics are unwarranted, however, in assuming that modern Chinese invocations of Huang's ideas reflect no more than the sentimental attachment of Chinese traditionalists to a past from which, against all rational calculation, they are reluctant to break their emotional ties. Even highly competent Japanese sinologues of the early twentieth century, both familiar with Chinese history and deeply concerned over the problems of modern China, have regarded Huang Zongxi as a major voice to be considered in the encounter between tradition and modernity.[13]

In present circumstances, if neither full freedom of public discourse nor electoral processes are likely prospects in the near term, the Chinese government still has need of educated men to serve the managerial elite, as well as to provide essential services in support of the modernization program to which it is committed. Can this be done without depending on schools, technical institutes, research centers, and scholarly academies, roughly the modern equivalent of Huang's schools and academies? If not, then is it unrealistic to think that such institutions, given the autonomy needed to do their work effectively, might not be able to serve as a kind of intermediate level or stage for the gradual expansion of a more liberal constitutional order? Indeed in some places and to some limited degree, such discussions are already taking place in the Chinese academy.

If the freedoms of expression and association are among the basic human rights, though never completely unqualified in practice, it is important to recognize that in Confucian tradition, too, public discussion *(gongyi)* was a recognized value, both in terms of the responsibility Confucian scholars felt to speak out against the abuse of power, and in terms of the increasing recognition by Neo-Confucians, culminating in the advocacy by Huang Zongxi, Lu Sheyi,[14] Lü Liuliang, and Tang Zhen in the seventeenth century, of duly constituted institutions to protect this public discussion (described by Huang in terms of laws and by Lü in terms of rites). One cannot, of course, claim this as a dominant political tradition in China; it does, however, constitute a significant line of Confucian thought from Confucius and Mencius down through Ouyang Xiu, the Cheng brothers, and Zhu Xi in the Song, as well as a number of Ming scholars from Fang Xiaoru down to the Donglin scholars of the sixteenth century and Huang Zongxi in the seventeenth century. On this basis one can call freedom of discussion and association a value recognized in Confucian tradition, however qualified its practice may have been by limiting circumstances in dynastic situations. And it stands in favorable contrast to the present situation in China, wherein freedom of thought is officially "recognized" but freedom of political association is not, with the consequence that the individual stands alone before all the power of the party and state.

Liang Qichao's Constitutionalism

In the late nineteenth century Liang Qichao (1873–1929)[15] was a disciple of Kang Youwei (1858–1927) and became his co-worker in the abortive Reform Movement of 1898, which attempted rapid, radical reforms in China's governance. After the failure of Kang's brief regime, Liang escaped to Japan and there became perhaps the most influential advocate of reform in the years before the Revolution of 1911. His writings, in a lucid and forceful style, dealt with a wide range of political, social, and cultural issues. To thousands of young Chinese studying abroad (most of them in Japan) or reading his books and pamphlets on the mainland, he became an inspiration and an idol—a patriotic hero, whose command of Chinese classical learning, together with a remarkable sensitivity to ideas and trends in the West, gave him the appearance of an intellectual giant joining Occident and Orient, almost a universal man.

Early on Liang joined Kang and Sun Yat-sen in the revival of Huang Zongxi's political ideas and in the reprinting of Huang's *Waiting for the Dawn* for circulation among reformist and republican circles at the turn of that century, both in China and Japan. While in exile, however, Liang published the fortnightly journal, *Renewing the People (Xinmin Congbao)*, from 1902 to 1905, which showed a significant change in his thinking in regard to "the people" as compared to the earlier views of both Zhu Xi and Huang Zongxi. Liang was now exposed far more to Western influences, and enormously impressed by Japan's progress in contrast to China's repeated failures. Sensing the power of nationalism as the force that galvanized the Western peoples and the Japanese into action, and realizing the apathy and indifference of China's millions towards the abortive palace revolution of 1898 (as, indeed, towards most public issues on the higher policy levels), Liang became fully convinced that popular education and the instillment of nationalism were China's greatest needs. In these years everything in her past culture that seemed an obstacle to national progress was to be cast aside. Nothing conveys this sense of a radical change better than the title of Liang's journal, *Renewing the People*.

Renewing the People

Anyone familiar with the Neo-Confucian curriculum ubiquitous in pre-modern East Asia would recognize that Liang's title draws upon the key expression, "renewing the people" in Zhu Xi's formulation of the Three Main Guidelines *(san gangling)* in the

Great Learning, first in order of his Four Books. Liang thereby establishes his own doctrine squarely in relation to the dominant philosophy of education in traditional China, but invests it with a new meaning. For Zhu Xi *xinmin* meant renewing the people through universal self-cultivation, as the basis of the whole social, political, and cultural order. Individual self-renewal would transform "the people" *(min)* and lift them up from an illiterate, undisciplined, inarticulate mass. Thus Zhu's key slogan: "Self-cultivation for the governance of men" *(xiuji zhiren).* In Liang's case, however, his sense of "a people" is of a "nation" informed by the Western (and Japanese) sense of nationalism. "A" people as a nation (not just "the" people as commoners) would become an organic group with a consciousness of its own identity, actively participating in the determination of its national destiny in a world of many contending peoples. To this end he sees a need for corporate organization, an educational system, and media of communication, bridging the gap between educated elite and illiterate masses. This involves not just individual self-understanding and self-cultivation, but one's own group learning from other peoples and their cultures.

At the same time, more than just responding to the challenge of Japan and the West, Liang is fleshing out the implications of Huang Zongxi's *Waiting for the Dawn: A Plan for the Prince.* Huang's most radical reformulation of Confucian political doctrine had been his moving beyond Mencius's and Hsun-tzu's stress on the people as the basis of the state (affirming, that is, the need for the consent of the governed) to the doctrine that the people should be active masters in the land and the ruler their servant. While Huang had expressed this principle in unmistakable language ("the people as masters," *min wei zhu*), the instrumentalities he proposed for effecting this had been limited to public discussion in the schools. In Huang's seventeenth-century circumstances even this arrangement would have represented a considerable advance (and in twentieth-century China too, it could be a step forward), but Liang now sensed that new instrumentalities in the West and Japan, such as public schools, publishing media, and societies for the advocacy of social, cultural, and political change) had given the people more effective means for joining in the political process. Through such means "the people" could become active participants in government—no longer just "subjects" or "commoners," reacting to the dictates of dynastic rulers, but a more self-conscious, alert, and engaged people comparable to the "citizens" of Western nations.

As Liang expressed it,

> The world of today is not the world of yesterday. In ancient times, we Chinese were people of villages instead of citizens. This is not because we were unable to form a citizenry, but due to circumstances. Since China majestically used to be the predominant power in the East, surrounded as we were by small barbarian groups and lacking any contact with other large states, we Chinese generally considered our state to encompass the whole world. All the messages we received, all that influenced our minds, all the instructions of our sages, and all that our ancestors passed down—qualified us to be individuals on our own, family members, members of localities and clans, and members of the world. But they did not qualify us to be citizens of a state. Although the qualifications of citizenship are not necessarily much superior to these other characteristics, in an age of struggle among nations for the survival of the fittest while the weak perish, if the qualities of citizens are wanting, then the nation cannot stand up independently between Heaven and Earth.
>
> If we wish to make our nation strong, we must investigate extensively the methods followed by other nations in becoming independent. We should select their superior points and appropriate them to make up for our own shortcomings . . . Thus, how to adopt and make up for what we originally lacked so that our people may be renewed should be deeply and carefully considered.
>
> *On Public Morality.* The main deficiency in our citizens is their lack of public morality. "Public morality" simply refers to that

which allows people to form groups and nations. Humans are the species of animal who can best establish themselves through this morality (as the Western philosopher Aristotle noted) . . .

Among our people there is not one who looks on national affairs as if they were his own affairs. The significance of public morality has not dawned on us . . .

Hence, we who live in the present group should observe the main trends of the world, study what will suit our nation, and create a new morality in order to solidify, benefit, and develop our group. We should not impose upon ourselves a limit and refrain from going into what our sages had not prescribed. Search for public morality and there will appear a new morality, there will appear "a people renewed."[16]

The Consciousness of Rights

Liang was aware that this new conception of a "people" as a "citizenry" carried with it a conception of "people's rights" new to the Chinese, which had to be explained. It meant that the "new citizenry" possessed rights both individually and collectively. The term here translated as "rights" is *quanli*, a more literal rendering of which would be "power and benefit" or "empowerment." The earliest use of the compound *quanli* occurs in the Confucian classic *Xunzi*, where we read that when one has perfected one's learning and self-cultivation, "*quanli* cannot move one [to do wrong]" (*Xunzi Index*, 3/1/49). In other words, Xunzi considered *quanli* to be a bad thing that we should not allow to influence us. Liang's essay on "Renewing the People" is representative of a movement towards reinterpreting and reevaluating *quanli* that was propelled both by internal Confucian developments and by Western writings (translated into Chinese terms by the Japanese) that emphasized rights as empowerment.

All people have responsibilities towards others that they ought to fulfill, and all people have responsibilities to themselves that they ought to fulfill. Not fulfilling one's responsibility to others is indirectly to harm the group, while not fulfilling one's responsibility to oneself is to directly harm the group . . . In giving birth to things, Heaven endowed them with innate abilities to defend and preserve themselves; all living things are examples of this. The reason why humans are superior to the other myriad things is that they have not only a "physical" existence, but also a "metaphysical" one. There is more than one requirement for metaphysical existence, but the most important of them is rights.

Where do rights originate? Rights originate in power or strength . . . For a human to be committed to strengthening himself through preserving his rights is an unparalleled method for firmly establishing and improving his group. In ancient Greece there were those who made offerings to the god of justice. The statue of this god held a scale in its left hand and sword in its right. The scale was for weighing rights and the sword was for protecting the practice of rights. To have a sword but no scale would be mean and wicked, but to have a scale without a sword is to make "rights" empty talk and ultimately futile . . .

The citizenry is an assemblage of individual persons. The rights of the state are composed of the rights of individuals. Therefore, the thoughts, feelings and actions of a citizenry will never be obtainable without the thoughts, feelings and actions of each individual member. That the people is strong means that the state is strong; that the people is weak means that the state is weak; that the people is rich means that the state is rich; that the people is poor means that the state is poor; that the people possesses rights means that the state possesses rights; and that the people is without shame means that the state is without shame . . .

The state is like a tree, and the consciousness of rights is like its roots. If the roots are destroyed, the tree will wither and die no matter how strong its trunk or vigorous its leaves . . . When a citizenry which lacks rights consciousness is confronted with foreign pressures, it is like a withered tree in a storm . . . I see that of all the millions of inhabitants of the earth, except for the black savages of India, Africa, and Southeast Asia, no one has a weaker sense of rights than do we Chinese.[17]

Liang Qichao's concept of a "new citizenry" and "public morality" was directly correlated to his new conviction concerning the nation as the irreducible core of social organization and civilized life. Like Sun Yat-sen, he believed that the Chinese lacked a sense of nationalism; traditional Chinese loyalties had been more to self and family. This left China without the solidarity and cohesion needed to survive in the struggle among nations. A conscious effort was therefore needed to develop a sense of nationhood and inculcate national loyalty among the people.

> Groups of people who form clans to live together and naturally create their own customs are called tribal peoples. People who have a concept of the nation and can participate in politics themselves are termed citizens. Nowhere on earth can nations be established without citizens . . .
>
> What does "being aware of the nation in relation to the individual" mean? Humanity is superior to other creatures in that people can form groups . . . Therefore, in regard to the internal domain . . . cooperative efforts make things easy and the division of labor benefits everybody, in that it is impossible for individuals to do everything by themselves. In regard to the outside world, at a time of crisis, the group combines all their wisdom and strength and defends the walls against invasion, while it is totally impossible for individuals to protect themselves. Thus did nations arise . . .
>
> We Chinese lack the concept of the nation. Inferior people only care about the prosperity of the individual and the family, while superior people airily deliberate philosophical truths, turning their backs on practical things . . .[18]

This issue arose for Liang in direct response to the challenge of modern nationalism, but it also reflects a sense (one shared with Sun Yat-sen, among others) that the Chinese traditionally were too individualistic, too centered on the self and family, and therefore lacked the sense of group loyalty and group participation necessary for asserting one's rights and fulfilling one's duties as citizens. Sun Yat-sen came to express this idea as the need of the Chinese not so much for freedom of the individual as for the "freedom of the nation."[19] Liang, however, was far more familiar with traditional Chinese culture, and especially Confucianism, than Sun, and his perception of the Chinese as too self-centered and lacking in group consciousness is a telling commentary on the views of modern writers who identify Confucianism with "communitarianism" and see the West as too individualistic. It is an even more telling commentary on the lack of an adequate civil infrastructure between the family/clan/lineage on the local level and the higher level on which, as Liang says, "superior people airily deliberate philosophical truths, turning their backs on practical things." The practical things, traditionally lacking, are what Liang calls the rights and responsibilities of citizens, which might have been secured by collective action on the intermediate level, between the self and family below and the universal state far above, but were neglected by "superior men" (the educated elite) discoursing on "airy philosophical truths," such as "bringing peace to all-under-Heaven," which were impractical dreams if unsupported by a working civil society.

If Liang is right in this perception, it means, as Huang Zongxi also implied, that the values enshrined in the Confucian rites, without the support of the communitarian structures advocated by more perceptive Confucians, were inadequate by themselves to cope with the problems of larger power structures and conflicts—hence the need for the "empowerment" of the people as rights-bearing citizens in an effective political infrastructure.

Liang's forced exile in Japan gave rise to one of the most important chapters in the development of a new Qing political journalism. Two of the most influential reform organs were founded in Japan by Liang Qichao in this period, *Qingyi bao* (*The China Discussion*, 1898), and *Xinmin congbao* (*New People's Miscellany*, 1902). This gave young intellectuals who later became major actors in the early twentieth-century China-based press an opportunity to develop their skills as reformists and publicists—skills that proved invaluable once reform was put back on the official agenda in Beijing, through an Imperial Decree of

January 29, 1901 that announced administrative reforms and opened up the possibility of more substantial political changes. Taking advantage of this opening, from the year 1904 reformists began to create newspapers and periodicals in China advocating the establishment of a constitutional monarchy. Their mission was to monitor the depth of the government's commitment to reform, encourage the development of politically aware constitutional citizens and guide China to a position of strength in the world through legal and institutional reform.[20]

While the Qing regime lasted, Liang remained in favor of constitutional monarchy, but after 1911 he accepted the new republican order. Thus when Yuan Shikai attempted a restoration of the monarchy in 1916, Liang refused to support it, contending consistently that the need to respect the established constitutional order transcended the claims of any authority figure. While many early advocates of modernization during and after World War I, like Yan Fu, experienced some disillusionment with the West and a loss of faith in wholesale Westernization, Liang sought increasingly to ground the modernization process in a strengthening of the rule of law and the building of a civil infrastructure, conducive to greater, informed participation of the people in government but also congenial to the more liberal of Chinese humanistic traditions.

7

Women's Education and Women's Rights

The sweeping change from a traditional curriculum to a Western style of education in 1905–1906 meant that the new generation had a better sense of world history than their predecessors but less acquaintance with China's past history and culture. One of the special strengths of Liang Qichao (as compared to the mostly Western-educated Sun Yat-sen) was his ability as a historian to relate old and new, and, perhaps chastened by his own personal experience of the failure in 1898 to accomplish rapid, wholesale change simply by Imperial decree, he spoke often of the need for continuity with the past, for gradual reform to build on whatever had enabled a people to survive into the present, rather than to push for too radical and sweeping an adoption of Western ideas and institutions. Thus even when writing about renewing the people, he said:

> What I mean by "renewing the people" is not being infatuated with Western ways and, in order to keep company with others, throwing away our own morals, learning, and customs of several thousand years' standing; nor is it to stick to old paper and say that merely embracing the morals, learning, and customs of these thousands of years will be sufficient for us to stand on the great earth . . . How to adopt and make up for what we originally lacked so that our people may be renewed, should be deeply and carefully considered.[1]

The new generation, however, was much less impressed with Chinese tradition than with the remarkable power and success of the West; they had little patience with the gradualism and sense of due process embodied in Liang's constitutionalism. If the latter can be classed as moderate, evolutionary, and even liberal (in the sense that it saw effective change as having to emerge from some organic growth process, rooted in the past rather than forcibly imposed from outside or above), the new attitude was radical, revolutionary, and liberationist.

It is ironical that many of China's leaders today should look back nostalgically to Confucian tradition, when the movement and party they still claim to represent was born of this radical, liberationist spirit, contemptuous of everything Confucian, and even consigning to the same Confucian dust-bin many evils that had no connection with it. The irony is especially apparent when we consider how early twentieth-century radicals called for liberation of the individual from the bonds of Confucian tradition. This is what one of the founders of the Chinese Communist Party, Chen Duxiu, had to say about it:

> In China, the Confucians have based their teachings on their ethical norms. Sons and wives possess neither personal individuality nor personal property. Fathers and elder brothers bring up their sons and younger brothers and are in turn supported by them. It is said in chapter 30 of the *Record of Rites* that "While parents are living, the son dares not regard his person or property as his own." [27:14] This is absolutely not the way to personal independence . . .
>
> Confucius lived in a feudal age. The ethics he promoted are the ethics of the feudal age. The social mores he taught and even his own mode of living were teachings and modes of a feudal age. The objectives, ethics, social norms, mode of living, and political institutions did not go beyond the privilege and prestige of a few rulers and aristocrats and had nothing to do with the happiness of the great masses . . .[2]

Now consider what was said even earlier by a leading feminist who championed a blend of anarchism and communism for the liberation of women:

The learning of Confucianism has tended to be oppressive and to promote male selfishness. Therefore, Confucianism marks the beginning of justifications for polygamy and chastity. People of the Han dynasty studied Confucianism and felt free to twist the meaning of the ancient writings as they pertained to women in order to extend their own views . . .

The ancients said that the relationship between the wife and her husband was like that of the minister and his ruler, and so men took precedence over women and men were honorable while women were contemptible. From this every evil theory designed to keep women from having freedom followed . . . Men were to Heaven as women were to earth and men were yang while women were yin. An absolute inequality was accordingly formed between men and women. Alas! . . .

Since men practiced polygamy and feared that women would want more than one husband, they therefore made women's morality a matter of diligence, chastity, and purity. They also feared that women would not be able to control themselves and so guided them with doctrines of prudence and staying at home; treating women like prisoners . . . Women [it was said] should die faithful to their deceased husbands, like a loyalist giving his life to his dynasty . . . Thus are women driven to their deaths with this empty talk of virtue. We can see that the Confucian insistence on propriety is nothing more than a tool for murdering women . . .

This proves that women have duties but no rights. Because household responsibilities cannot be assumed by men, all the tasks of managing the household are given to women. Out of fear that women might interfere with their concerns, men made up the theory that women had no business outside of the home . . . Keeping women at home allowed men to pursue education while women were trapped in ignorance. Isn't this the greatest of injustices? . . .

Therefore, since this doctrine has been propagated by the Confucians, not only have men enjoyed and followed it but also women have sincerely believed in it. Not only has it harmed scholarship but it has also harmed the law . . . The laws are based on the doctrine that men are superior while women are base. The law was thus based on scholarship while scholarship was based on Confucian writings. If we do not utterly abolish the false doctrines of the Confucian writings, the truth will never again be heard.[3]

It is perhaps not surprising, given the chaotic circumstances and traumatizing events attendant on the fall of the Qing dynasty in 1911, that young intellectuals should have been so quick to disown their own past in such sweeping language. It is understandable too that these bitter complaints should, in turn, have become subject to more recent revisionist review by writers who consider them to have been grossly overdrawn and far from a just appraisal of Confucian tradition. But before we propose a different, historical perspective, or dismiss these early twentieth-century critiques as simply born of frustration or fevered imaginings, reflective of disjointed times, let us consider similar but earlier observations by a foreigner, whose judgments could hardly have been tainted by the rash impatience of modern liberationists or feminists. They came from a French Catholic missionary, Abbé Huc, who traveled extensively in China during the 1840s and whose travel diaries showed him to be fair and judicious on the whole in trying to represent Chinese customs and institutions for Western readers. Largely untouched by modern liberal sentiments and biases, Huc nevertheless was unequivocal in his condemnation of the treatment of women in China. Though his recital of the injustices they suffered is too lengthy and detailed to be reproduced here, his book may be hard for some readers to come by today, so I hope the sense of it may be gotten from the following passages:

The condition of Chinese women is most pitiable; suffering, privation, contempt, all kinds of misery and degradation, seize on her in the cradle, and accompany her pitilessly to the tomb. Her very birth is commonly regarded as a humiliation and a disgrace to the family—an evident sign of the malediction of Heaven. If she be not immediately suffocated (according to an atrocious custom that we shall speak of by and by), she is regarded and treated as a creature radically despicable and scarcely belonging to the human race . . .

This public and private servitude of women—a servitude that opinion, legislation, manners, have sealed with their triple seal—has become, in some measure, the cornerstone of Chinese society. The young girl lives shut up in the house where she was born, occupied exclusively with the cares of housekeeping, treated by everybody, and especially by her brothers, as a menial, from whom they have a right to demand the lowest and most painful services. The amusements and pleasures of her age are quite unknown to her; her whole education consists in knowing how to use her needle; she neither learns to read nor to write; there exists for her neither school nor house of education; she is condemned to vegetate in the most complete and absolute ignorance, and no one ever thinks of, or troubles himself about her, till the time arrives when she is to be married . . .

The young girl is simply an object of traffic, an article of merchandise to be sold to the highest bidder, without her having the right to ask a single question concerning the merit or quality of her purchaser. On the day of the wedding there is great anxiety to adorn and beautify her. She is clad in splendid robes of silk, glittering with gold and jewels; her beautiful plaits of raven hair are ornamented with flowers and precious stones; she is carried away in great pomp, and musicians surround the brilliant palanquin, where she sits in state like a queen on her throne. You think, perhaps, on witnessing all this grandeur and rejoicing, that now, at last, her period of happiness is about to begin. But, alas! a young married woman is but a victim adorned for the sacrifice. She is quitting a home where, however neglected, she was in the society of the relations to whom she had been accustomed from her infancy. She is now thrown, young, feeble, and inexperienced, among total strangers, to suffer privation and contempt, and be altogether at the mercy of her purchaser.

This picture of the unrelieved misery and degradation of Chinese women yields finally to a very different picture when Abbé

Huc describes the situation of those brought up in Chinese Christian families:

> The recovery of women in China from this abject state is going on slowly, it is true, but in a most striking and effectual manner. In the first place, it need hardly be said that the little girl born in a Christian family is not murdered, as is often the case among the pagans. Religion is there to watch over her at her birth, to take her lovingly in its arms, and say, "Here is a child created in the image of God, and predestined, like you, to immortality . . ."
>
> The young Christian girl is not permitted to stagnate in ignorance; she does not vegetate, forsaken by everyone, in a corner of the paternal mansion; for since she must learn her prayers and study the Christian doctrine, it is necessary to renounce in her favor the most inveterate prejudices of her nation. Schools must be founded for her, where she may be enabled to develop her intellect, to learn in the books of her religion those mysterious characters which are for other Chinese women an inexplicable enigma. She will be in the society of numerous companions of her own age; and at the same time that her mind is becoming enlarged and her heart formed to virtue, she will learn in some measure in what consists the life of this world.
>
> It is more especially by marriage contracted in the Christian form that the Chinese woman shakes off the frightful servitude of pagan customs, and enters on the rights and privileges of the great family of humanity . . .
>
> The Christian women also always possess in their families the influence and the prerogatives of wives and mothers; and it may be observed that they enjoy greater liberty out of doors. The practice of assembling on Sundays and festival days at chapels and oratories to pray in common, and be present at the divine offices, creates and maintains relations of intimacy among them. They go out oftener to visit each other, and form from time to time those little social parties which are so useful in dissipating care and vexation, and in helping one to support the burden of life. Pagan women know nothing of these comforts and consolations; they were almost always secluded, and nobody cares if they wear out their souls in languor and ennui.[4]

Now before attempting an assessment of these sweeping critiques of the treatment of women in traditional China, I should like to turn to some of the classic texts that might help to clarify the actual relationship of Confucianism historically to some of the points at issue.

Critiques of Confucianism in the early twentieth century frequently targeted the concept of the Three Bonds *(sangang)* as the source of much evil done to women. "Bonds" is not perhaps an inappropriate translation for *gang* (more literally, the "mainstays" of a net) since "bond" can be read either in the sense of "bonding" or "bondage," and both senses of the word had come into play by the twentieth century. The Three Bonds are ruler/minister, parent/child, and husband/wife. Some Confucian writers have stressed the last of these relations as primary, because without husband and wife there could be no children, and without the parent/child relation there would be no moral or spiritual basis (understood in this case as filial piety) for the ruler/minister to rest on.

Zhu Xi and most Neo-Confucians, however, follow the Five Relations as found in *Mencius* that, as we have seen in chapter 1, begin with the parent/child relation and stress intimate affection as the fundamental basis of all human relations. Indeed Zhu Xi rarely mentions the Three Bonds—not surprising since the *sangang* have no place in the Confucian classics, and were only codified later in Han texts (a fact that may explain why He Zhen, in the passage quoted just before that of Abbé Huc, speaks of "Confucians, representing the ancestral learning of the Han dynasty, [who] felt free to twist the meaning of the ancient writings as they pertain to women in order to extend their own views"). Thus, if one looks for the meaning and significance of the Three Bonds, which lack any firm basis in Confucian scripture, one is shooting at an historically moving target, at a concept inherently subject to later adaptation and alteration.

Although the Three Bonds, of Legalist provenance, are men-tioned briefly by the Confucian Dong Zhongshu in the Former Han period, the prime basis for an understanding of their original content is the first-century CE text of *Discourses in the White Tiger Hall (Bohudong delun)*, which attempted to define Confucian teachings for that time. As recorded by the eminent historian Ban Gu (32–92 CE), these discussions on the Classics and on Confucian themes held at the imperial court are typical of the process by which Confucianism became codified through state patronage of classical scholarship linked to public morality. The priority given to state over family loyalties (ruler/minister first) is one sign of this. Other signs are the coordination of those relations with hierarchies in nature such as the triadic order of Heaven, Earth and Humankind, the succession of the Five Phases and the yin-yang dualism—all more characteristic of Han thought than of Zhou.

Yet if the yin-yang relationship can be seen as assertive on the part of the male and recessive on that of the female, the *Bohudong* account of these relations also stresses their complementary nature: "Why is it that although ruler and minister, parent and child, husband and wife are altogether six people, they are referred to as Three Mainstays? Because the alternation of yin and yang constitute one Way. The yang completes itself by obtaining the yin; the yin finds order in the yang, the firm and soft complement each other. Therefore the six people make up Three Mainstays."[5]

Thus it is union and combination that Ban Gu stresses, not separate individual roles. Moreover, in this context the relation of husband and wife is portrayed as essentially creative, which, as with the interaction of yin and yang, serves the procreation of humankind. Yet in combination they are also seen as mutually supportive, a characteristic also of the parent/child relationship, which, perhaps surprisingly for modern readers, speaks not only of the parent instructing the child but of the child admonishing the parent. Thus it quotes the *Classic of Filial Piety:* "If a father has a remonstrating son it will keep him from wrong-doing." And as a matter of fact the *Classic of Filial Piety* itself is emphatic on this point. Following is the dialogue it attributes to Confucius and his disciple Zengzi:

> Zengzi said: "I have heard your instructions concerning affection and loving respect, comforting one's parents and upholding one's good name. May I presume to ask, if a child follows all of his parents commands, can this be called filiality?"
>
> The Master replied, "What kind of talk is this! What kind of talk is this! Of old the Son of Heaven had seven counsellors, so that even if he himself lost the Way, he still would not lose his sway over all-under-Heaven . . . If a father even had one son to remonstrate with him, he still would not fall into evil ways. In the face of whatever is not right, the son cannot but remonstrate with his father, and the minister cannot but remonstrate with his prince. If it is not right, remonstrate! . . ."

Ban Gu's sister, Ban Zhao (45?–116? CE), herself a distinguished scholar from a leading scholarly family, is responsible for the first "classic" of women's education: *Admonitions for Women (Nujie),* later included as the first in the Ming period compilation of the *Four Books for Women.* On the whole Ban Zhao's precepts, written for her daughters, confirm the picture of the womanly virtues as those of gentleness, modesty, purity, industry, patient endurance, and service of her husband and family—not at all unlike the characterization of the submissive wife given in the feminist He Zhen's protest quoted above. But there is more.

Husband and wife must be worthy of each other in their respective roles:

> If a husband be unworthy, then he possesses nothing by which to control his wife. If a wife be unworthy, she possesses nothing by which to serve her husband . . . In practice these two work out in the same way . . . But now examine the gentlemen of

the present age. They only know that wives must be controlled and the husband's authority must be maintained. They therefore teach their boys to read books and study histories, but they do not know how husbands and masters are to be served, or how rites and right principles are to be maintained. Yet only to teach men and not to teach women—is this not ignoring the reciprocal relation between them? According to the *Rites,* book learning begins at the age of eight [seven by Western count], and at fifteen [fourteen by Western count] one goes off to school. Why, however, should this principle not apply to girls as well as to boys?[6]

Ban Zhao does not put a fine point on it, but the clear implication is of a reciprocity that should not only provide "book learning" for girls in the home but schooling for them away from home after the age of fifteen *(sui)*! In time girls in better homes did learn to read and often became the first instructors of boys in the home, but to have schools for girls was almost unheard of down into the twentieth century. But in the first century CE, Ban Zhao is raising a key point in the Confucian principle of reciprocity: Why would it tolerate for so long this inequality between the sexes? Regardless of any comparison to other cultures (which would not necessarily be unfavorable to China), this is a fair question to raise within the context of the tradition itself, to be answered, if it can be, on the basis of standards internal to it.

Ban Zhao's text later became the prototype of other instructional texts for women, and she became canonized as the archetypal female wisdom figure, so much so that other texts in this genre adopt Ban Zhao's voice rather than their own.

In the Tang period the two most popular Confucian texts were the *Analects* of Confucius and the *Classic of Filial Piety;* thus it is not surprising that the authors of two instructional texts for women written in this period should draw on the titles of these texts, namely the *Analects for Women (Nü Lunyu)* and the *Classic of Filial*

Piety for Women (Nü Xiaojing). Much of the latter text details how women should serve their husbands and parents-in-law, how the spirit of respectfulness engendered by filial piety should even apply to one's kindly treatment of other relatives (younger wives, sister-in-laws, and so on), as well as of servants and even chickens and dogs. But the most striking feature is its amplification of the original Classic's duty of remonstration:

> The women said [supposedly to Ban Zhao], "We dare to ask whether if we follow all our husbands' commands, we could be called virtuous?"
>
> Her Ladyship answered, "What kind of talk is that! What kind of talk is that! Long ago, King Xuan of Zhou was late rising to attend his court, so his wife threw down her jewels in the public tribunal [to take the blame]. King Xuan, because of this, started getting up early again. Emperor Cheng of the Han ordered his concubine to ride out with him, but she refused, saying, 'I have heard that in the Three Dynasties, wise rulers took only their worthy officials by their side. I never heard of them taking their concubines.' Because of her, Emperor Cheng changed his manner . . .
>
> "From these cases, we can see that if the Son of Heaven has ministers to advise him, even if he is neglectful of the Way, he won't lose his empire. If a lord has remonstrating officials, then even if he is neglectful of the Way, he won't lose his state. If a great officer has someone to remonstrate with him, then even if he is neglectful of the Way, he won't lose his home domain. If a scholar has a remonstrating friend, then he can't be parted from his good name. If a father has a remonstrating son, then he won't fall prey to what is against moral standards. If a husband has a remonstrating wife then he won't fall into evil ways. Therefore if a husband transgresses against the Way, you must correct him. How could it be that to obey your husband in everything would make you a virtuous person?" . . .[7]

It is clearly implied in such admonitions that the woman cannot be thought, and certainly cannot think of herself, as merely a submissive servant of her husband. She must be a mature person, capable of independent judgment and in full control of herself (even if within certain defined and limiting circumstances). The same is largely true of the other Tang dynasty work, the *Analects for Women,* by two daughters of a high official, one of whom did not marry but dedicated herself to the instruction of women at court (Song Ruozhao). From this one can see that her concept of womanhood allowed her to define for herself a social role and vocation independent of the wifely role. Nevertheless, her instructions themselves focus mainly on duties within the family and household, and confirm what is generally true of such instructions—that the woman's role is seen as the wifely role.

Within that context, however, Song Ruozhao spells out in detail her duties and responsibilities: the wife is called upon to be a real manager, and not merely a gentle, soft, yielding female. In this respect the *Analects for Women* confirms that, depending upon her individual capacities, the wife and mother in many Chinese households was often a strong, assertive manager, and, in the domestic realm, a partner (albeit junior in theory) in a common enterprise, rather than just a meek and passive servant of the male.

The last of the Four Books carries this genre to another altogether unique and remarkable level. It is *Instructions for the Inner Quarters (Neixun),* by the Empress Xu, consort of the third Ming emperor, but also a protégé of the first Ming empress. At a time when Neo-Confucian teachings were giving a vital impetus to education, Empress Xu became dissatisfied with the conventional literature available for the cultivation of women, and aimed to produce a guide of her own based on the personal instruction she had received from her mother-in-law, the Empress Ma,[8] wife of the dynasty's founder, Ming Taizu. In contrast to the stereotype of the arbitrary and abusive mother-in-law in China, Empress Ma was much admired by the later Empress Xu as a firm but humane and sympathetic mentor.

As a peasant woman married early to Taizu before his rise to power, the future Empress Ma was, like him, largely self-educated and eventually quite well read (not an altogether uncommon thing in traditional China, for many women did overcome the handicap imposed by a lack of formal schooling, just as Ming Taizu himself did). Moreover, as empress with several daughters-in-law under her charge, she conducted regular study groups on the classics for the women of the palace.

Taizu himself, as we have seen, was well known for his despotic rule, his hot temper, his violence and cruelty, his bloody purges, and his suspiciousness and vindictiveness towards any who opposed him or whom he suspected of treason. Yet there are numerous stories about how Empress Ma remonstrated with and restrained him, saving the lives of many unjustly accused. Such was the case when Taizu turned against one of his foremost Neo-Confucian advisers, Song Lian,[9] and ordered his execution. Empress Ma defended Song and got his sentence reduced to exile. In another significant case, when Taizu complained about Empress Ma's interference in state affairs, she refused to back off, saying that just as he had responsibilities as Father of the Country, so was she as its Mother entitled to be concerned about the welfare of her children. Thus she turned the family/state analogy into one which set paternal and maternal care nearly on a par, with the latter a definite counterweight to the former. Empress Ma, by the way, died a natural death after many others in the emperor's service had suffered unnatural ones, and she was said to have been deeply mourned by Taizu, who did not replace her as empress.

Empress Ma's view of her larger social responsibilities seems to have taken deep root in the consciousness of Empress Xu, and pervades virtually all of the *Instructions for the Inner Quarters,* at each successive stage of which the "inner" or restricted conception of a woman's role gives way to a more expansive one. For anyone with a sensitivity to its Neo-Confucian meanings, the *Neixun* may be recognized as far from a rehash of conventional views about the place of women in the home. Indeed the very structure and thematic development of the work are reminiscent of the Neo-Confucian genre of instruction to rulers and noblemen as found in Zhu Xi's memorials and lectures to the emperor, his *Reflections on Things at Hand, Elementary Learning* and commentary on the *Great Learning,* and Zhen Dexiu's "Lectures from the Classics Mat," as well as the latter's monumental *Extended Meaning of the Great Learning.*

The opening portion deals with women's self-cultivation. Yet, instead of leading off with a gendered presentation of the strictly defined role of the woman (and most often of the wife in the home), the prior basis established here for any such role-playing or modeling is the making of a human self and shaping of a human life, based on the Neo-Confucian principle of the shared moral nature in all human beings: "If you do not cultivate your own moral character, then your chances of managing your own family will be slim, how much less your bringing order into the world" (3:7a). From this the work goes on to many specific prescriptions on how this cultivation is to be accomplished in the woman's case, paralleling what is set forth for men in Zhu's *Elementary Learning.* Yet the Empress's thought that a woman should undertake these with the ultimate goal of "bringing order into the world" suggests how far beyond the confines of the home goes her aspiration for Neo-Confucian education.

Subsequent chapters cite historical examples of women who played major roles in assisting founders of dynasties and great rulers in governing well (much as Fan Ziyu's *Learning of the Emperors* credits great scholar-mentors in similar roles). The standout case is, of course, Empress Ma. With such models to emulate, it is not too much, says Empress Xu, for women to aspire even to sagehood. Contrary to a widespread view that only men could achieve this goal, Empress Xu argues that all humans, female as well as male, have the same innate Heavenly endowment of a moral nature, which represents the potential for sagehood. It is a gift not just to certain specially favored persons or just to men, but something anyone could hope to achieve through learning—echoing the assertion of Zhou Dunyi in his *Tongshu*, and prominently quoted in Zhu Xi's *Reflections on Things at Hand (Jinsilu)*, that sagehood can be learned and should be striven for by all.

It would be rash to draw too many conclusions from the limited evidence represented by the texts discussed above, but a few useful observations may be made.

Each of the texts cited offers insights into the condition of women and their potential for something better than the conventional picture of their depressed condition has allowed for. Nevertheless, the perspectives opened up here only balance that picture; they do not contradict or cancel out what was reported by Abbé Huc or He Zhen.

The female authors of these texts all speak from a somewhat privileged position, either because they share to some degree in the higher culture of scholar-official families or because they have risen from commoner status to positions of special advantage (e.g. the Empresses Ma and Xu). From such vantage points they see both possibilities and problems of an unusual sort. For instance, they see the implications of Confucian and especially Neo-Confucian ethical doctrines that ordinary women would be less conscious of, if at all, with regard to a more public role. Still, as the title of Empress Xu's text indicates, she is offering "instructions for the inner quarters," that is, from within the defined context of women's household role. It is only in her case, as in Empress Ma's, that the role is played out on a larger stage, at which the complementary relationship of husband/wife engages the latter in some of her mate's responsibilities as ruler. To meet the demands of wifely complementarity and reciprocity at this stage requires of Empress Xu a greater sense of personhood, which Zhu Xi's Four Books and other basic Neo-Confucian texts speak to in a new and special way, applicable to both men and women.

Although the discourse has thus been raised to a new level in this latter case, it leaves unanswered the key question raised much earlier by Ban Zhao with respect to the inequality of women and lack of reciprocity in education. Confucian reciprocity has served certain purposes but not others. As we have seen in the cases of Lü Kun and Chen Hongmou (cited in chapter 4), some leading Confucian scholar-officials, aware of this incongruity between humane ideals and the invidious discrimination against women in the matter of education, proposed to remedy it, but without much success.

In the light of these observations one can understand the protests of He Zhen in the twentieth century. She speaks to unresolved questions deep in the culture itself, to which she has been awakened by a new awareness of possibilities presented by Western civilization for the enlargement of women's role, especially in the public sphere to which, until now, women had only been adjunct as wives in privileged situations. Whether a further internal evolution of Chinese society and Confucian thought might, on its own, have brought a resolution of this issue without intervention from outside, is a matter for speculation. In any event the course of world history determined that in this matter, as in Liang Qichao's realization of the need for constitutional government and the essential elements of a civil society, substantial change would await outside intervention.

8

Chinese Communism and Confucian Communitarianism

As we may judge from Chinese historical experience, the recent promotion of "Asian values" is not the first attempt to appropriate certain Confucian concepts for authoritarian purposes. And this pattern repeated itself in the early twentieth century. For all the anti-Confucian rhetoric of the Chinese Communist movement, and the fundamental differences between "Mao Zedong thought" and Confucianism, Mao and his comrades were still glad to avail themselves of whatever moral idealism survived from traditional Chinese political culture. The Neo-Confucian attitudes of "taking responsibility oneself" *(ziren)* for "saving the world" *(qiushi),* so pronounced a feature of the later Wang Yangming school to which Mao was early exposed, lent itself, stripped of Zhu Xi's caution and prudential rationalism, to messianic causes, and in Mao's case to the kind of revolutionary enthusiasm he sought to enkindle among the youthful Red Guards as the vanguard of the Cultural Revolution.

Among the Red Guards this revolutionary idealism was meant to recreate the kind of zeal that had once inspired the activism and self-sacrificing struggle of Mao's earlier revolutionary campaigns, at which time Mao's trusted aide, Liu Shaoqi, had written a guide, *How to Be a Good Communist,* for the ideological rectification of Party cadres. The original title of the work in Chinese was more literally "The Cultivation of Communist Party Members," the language of which, as well as references in the text itself, suggest a conscious evocation of Confucian methods of self-cultivation as models for cadres to emulate. From Liu's account one can readily identify his main source as that ubiquitous text of late Neo-Confucian education and self-reformation, the *Great Learning*, which we have encountered again and again as a pivotal text for key figures from Zhu Xi down through Xu Heng and Wang Yangming to Liang Qichao. But there are also references to specific Neo-Confucian practices of "daily renewal" by which one was reminded (in the language of the *Great Learning* and the *Mean*) to "Watch over oneself when alone"; that is, to monitor one's own thought and actions and measure one's self-improvement from day to day. As Liu put it:

> In ancient China, there were many methods of cultivation. There was Zeng Zi who said: "I reflect on myself three times a day." The *Classic of Odes* has it that one should cultivate oneself "as a lapidary cuts and files, carves and polishes." Another method was "to examine oneself by self-reflection" and to "write down some mottoes on the right-hand side of one's desk" or "on one's girdle" as daily reminders of rules of personal conduct. The Chinese scholars of the Confucian school had a number of methods for cultivation of their body and mind. Every religion has various methods and forms of cultivation of its own. The "investigation of things, the extension of knowledge, sincerity of thought, the rectification of the heart, the cultivation of the person, the regulation of the family, the ordering well of the state and bringing peace to all-under-Heaven" as set forth in the *Great Learning* also mean the same. All this shows that in achieving one's progress one must make serious and energetic efforts to carry on self-cultivation and study.[1]

What appeals to Liu in this formulation is the focus on moral voluntarism and self-correction, on the direct activation of the moral will, with the possibility this offers of generating in party cadres a strong sense of personal responsibility for and zealous commitment to militant struggle. Liu is aware, however, that the

Neo-Confucian method is deeply introspective and requires quiet reflection. Therefore, so as to avoid a misunderstanding and miscarriage of the enterprise, he adds:

> However, many of these methods and forms cannot be adopted by us because most of them are idealistic, formalistic, abstract, and divorced from social practice. These scholars and religious believers exaggerate the function of subjective initiative, thinking that so long as they keep their general "good intentions" and are devoted to silent prayer they will be able to change the existing state of affairs, change society, and change themselves under conditions separated from social and revolutionary practice. This is, of course, absurd. We cannot cultivate ourselves in this way. We are materialists and our cultivation cannot be separated from practice.[2]

The misconceived reference here to "silent prayer" probably points to the Neo-Confucian meditative practice of "quiet-sitting" *(jingzuo)*, meant to straighten and steady the mind as a prelude to right action, but instead taken here by Liu as harboring a dangerous tendency to lapse into quiet self-reflection and passivity.

Yet in itself this contemplative practice points to the same critical self-consciousness and moral self-awareness in Confucian personalism that early twentieth-century writers have already complained about as too individualistic and a danger to the common cause—prejudicial in their case to nationalism, but in Liu's case to class struggle led by the Communist Party. The necessary corrective to this subjective idealism is, for Liu, self-criticism in the context of Party struggle meetings. The Party's guidance, elsewhere defined in terms of the process of "democratic centralism" rather than obedience to one's own conscience (the mind of the Way implanted in one's nature, according to Zhu Xi and Wang Yangming), would provide the criteria by which one could check and correct one's own wayward or selfish impulses and become fully engaged with the larger cause. In Liu's words:

What is important to us is that we must not under any circumstances isolate ourselves from the revolutionary struggles of different kinds of people . . . Our self-cultivation and self-steeling are for no other purpose than that of revolutionary practice. That is, we must modestly try to understand the standpoint, method, and spirit of Marx-Leninism, and understand how Marx, Engels, Lenin, and Stalin dealt with people . . . Moreover, we should stick to them and unreservedly correct and purge everything in our own identity that runs counter to them . . . At all times and on all questions, a Communist Party member should take into account the interests of the Party as a whole, and place the Party's interest above his personal problems and interests. It is the highest principle of our Party members that the Party's interests are supreme.[3]

In this instance we see both continuity and radical change in the perception—if not distortion—of the Confucian legacy. Self-examination is translated into self-rectification at the hands of the Party, and its links to a universalist ideal ("bringing peace to all-under-Heaven" as the *Great Learning*'s ultimate goal) have been transferred to world revolutionary struggle. In the process Confucianism is sloughed off by Liu as an anachronism, as "subjective individualism" (despite this, Liu would later be accused by Mao of promoting "Confucian individualism" through this work).[4] The transition—or rather the leap, as in Mao's Great Leap of 1958—seems disarmingly easy because the paradigm of the *Great Learning* itself, as we saw earlier, is vague concerning the intermediate stage we have identified as the community—the civil interface between family and state. Mao's communes might have bridged this gap, but as instruments of state power and control they lacked the autonomy to serve a genuine communitarian function.

Indeed it was precisely in this respect that the communes failed. Instead of being truly voluntaristic and cooperative organizations, which might have served the purposes of genuine communication between the people and the state, they were instruments of state control. When the Great Leap failed, Mao had difficulty getting information he could rely on about the actual situation at ground level. Even though he deputized committees to go into the countryside and study the actual conditions there, he could not trust their reports, either because people were afraid to speak out, because factional interests and rivalries prejudiced the results, or because the insecurities of party and state officials led them to falsify or suppress the facts. Communes imposed from above, no matter how camouflaged by the pretense of popular, grassroots demand, could not overcome the credibility gap, and Mao was left the victim of his own preconceptions—not alone his indomitable conviction that the communes were the final solution to China's problems, but that he knew best how to "go to the people," instead of letting them come to him. Liu Shaoqi and the Party were caught in much the same trap.[5]

Now, despite Deng's liberalization of the economy, there has still been no significant relaxation of the party's monopolization of the political process. Hence, in the terms we have been using here, statism (the Party dictatorship) has asserted itself once again, and stands as the substantive reality behind (as well as in ironical contrast to) any claim of the present leadership to represent a communitarian social order.

Still, this is not the whole story or the final chapter as far as Confucianism is concerned, and if any among the present leadership wish to have their claim to speak for Confucianism taken seriously, they will have to acknowledge that there are others with a more authentic and consistent claim to represent this tradition than they. And among several who might so qualify as genuine Confucians, I would cite the case of Liang Shuming as particularly illustrative of our problem here.

At a time when Confucianism was being decried as decadent and outmoded, Liang Shuming (1893–1988) endorsed it as the basis for a reconstruction of Chinese civilization and later too for world civilization. Though not unappreciative of certain Western values, such as individualism and science, that might be embraced in a synthesis with China's own humanistic values, he condemned wholesale Westernization as impractical and undesirable. Instead he believed that underlying traditional values and orientations would constitute a more practical basis for building a cohesive modern society, as well as the basis for a future human culture. A sound program of reconstruction, Liang believed, could start only at the grassroots and slowly evolve into a new society, avoiding the excesses of both capitalism and Communism.

To promote such reconstruction of agriculture and rural life, Liang founded the Shandong Rural Reconstruction Institute. He was one of the founders of the Democratic League and was prominent in the attempt to mediate between the Nationalist and Communist parties after World War II. Later, under the pressure of Communist ideological campaigns, he steadfastly refused to confess any errors.

Reconstructing the Community

The following excerpts are from Liang's "Reconstruction of the Village Community." In it he addresses the problem of community organization by reference to the original community compact *(xiangyue)* advocated by Zhu Xi on the basis of his reconstruction of the earlier compact of the Lü family in the eleventh century. In the form recommended by Zhu and adapted later by Wang Yangming and other sixteenth-and seventeenth-century Neo-Confucian reformers, Liang saw a type of voluntary, cooperative organization that could be adapted to modern needs, but would avoid the passivity of the authoritarian, bureaucratic "village lecture" system officially established under the Ming and Qing. In this Liang reflected a consciousness shared by many earlier twentieth-century reformers that traditional China was riven by a gap between the top-heavy power structure above and a fragmented, individualistic, politically inert society below. In other words, he was addressing the lack of a more active and involved infrastructure such as that which we have called "civil society." The following precis of his ideas is drawn from translations by Catherine Lynch.[6]

> In simple terms, we can indicate two points: one, the question of science and technology, and two, the question of group organization. As for science and technology, everyone has seen how the West is superior and how we are deficient . . . What I want to discuss now is the question of group organization.
>
> Westerners have always had everywhere group life, beginning from religion and on to economics and government, whereas Chinese have always lacked group life. Everywhere it seems the whole is broken into parts . . .[7]
>
> What is meant by construction is nothing but the construction of a new structure of social organization; that is, to construct new customs. Why? Because in the past our structure of social organization was shaped out of social customs; it was not shaped out of national laws . . .[8]
>
> In the contemporary world, if the Chinese do not move toward group organization, in the future they will not be able to exist. Reality compels us towards organization, to turn in the direction of the West . . . but might this in turn be incompatible with our old spirit? . . . Although Chinese lack group organization, they are not opposed to group organization, hence there is no necessary conflict.[9]

From this one can see that Liang Shuming avoids the facile, simplistic resolution of the problem in a way that pits Asia or China against the West, with the former seen as upholding the needs of the group, and the West as promoting unrestrained individual freedom. China may even turn to the West for a certain type of group organization that it lacks, and while doing so, acquire a measure of the individual freedom needed to overcome the passivity that enervated and vitiated the community compact in its Ming and Qing incarnation. As the following passages make clear, this change need not mean that China would abandon its traditional forms of personal and social relations, as cited in our initial paradigm, but only supplement them in compatible ways.

> This is a time of great distress for the Chinese, a time caught in contradiction on either side, coming and going. That is to say, on the one hand the Chinese lack group organization, and at the same time they lack the establishment of individual liberty and equality; the two [deficiencies] both urgently await being made up. But if we emphasize the aspect of liberty and equality . . . then it will be very difficult for us to attend to the aspect of combining into groups and will cause the Chinese to be even more dispersed.
>
> [R]egarding the group organization we have just discussed, the principle of this organization is based in China's idea of ethics. It is as if, to the five relationships of parent/child, ruler/minister, husband/wife, elder brother/younger brother, and friends, there were added a relationship of group towards member, member towards group . . .[10]
>
> The community compact was a bit inactive; we want to change it to be active . . . Earlier the Chinese did not much look for progress in their mode of life. For example, having hand carts and ox and horse carts, they could neglect to strive for cars and trains. This kind of attitude is also evident in the community compact. We, on the other hand, will change it into something active, encompassing the sense of striving for progress in active undertakings . . .

If Liang sees Western forms of group organization as providing for, and indeed calling for, a greater measure of individual freedom, this is needed because the type of individualism that hampered China in the past was in fact too limiting. It was defined in terms of static roles and relationships, and of norms that failed to recognize, he says, the open-endedness of goodness. Its concept of humanity or humaneness needed to be expressed in a more expansive conception of the social enterprise. In the following,

Liang refers to the limited scope of the traditional community compact, but no doubt he is also thinking of the paradigm of Neo-Confucian self-cultivation that culminates in, and is capped by, the *Great Learning's* "resting in the utmost good" (*zhih yu zhih shan*); that is, the Mean.

> Our judgment is that earlier Chinese, in the community compact, overly emphasized the goodness [*shan*] of the individual, how to perfect the moral character of the individual. Regarding the ideal of goodness, it seems to have been a bit limited, as if goodness were not in an endless course of unfolding. That is to say, in the compact of the earlier Chinese, one can discern that they harbor a customary standard and think that it is enough to reach this standard. In fact goodness is inexhaustible, always in the course of unfolding. Yet in the [earlier] community compact it was as if there were a set standard, and as if it leaned towards individual goodness. Its defects were leaning towards the individual and being limited. Our supplementing transformation is to regard society in place of the emphasis on the individual, to see an endless unfolding in place of what is limited . . .
>
> Our community compact is not just the compact of a single village; it is not that those in one village can encourage each other to goodness and that is sufficient . . . From connecting village with village, we want gradually to reach to the connection of county with county, province with province; to make connections everywhere, to have mutual intercourse, to communicate information . . . If we want to transform society, then we as individuals are unable to transform it; it is necessary to make connections . . .[11]
>
> In the practice of the community compact, relying on political power will not work, promotion by private individuals also will not work . . . We understand that to rely on political power to do things—to use the power of command and coercion, if this kind of power is used, in each step it all is mechanical . . .
>
> We want to stir up aspiration, place economics in this kind of human life, allow human life to drive economics, control economics, enjoy the use of economics, not to cause economics to

control human life. (Among Westerners, it is economics that controls human life.) If we want to accomplish this, then it is all the more a question of spirit, a question of human life or, we could say, a question of culture.[12]

To sum up Liang's argument, we may cite the main points as follows: (1) To modernize and cope with the West, China urgently needs a new kind of group organization. (2) This could be rooted in the community compact as originally developed in the Song and Ming on a voluntary basis, but must break out of self-limiting norms and avoid the stultifying type of compact dominated by a state that did not encourage individual initiative. (3) The Chinese, though in some ways too individualistic, need to develop a greater individual liberty and equality that is grounded in community organization and aspires to participate in a larger human community. (4) Human relations in the community compact can be seen as an extension of the traditional Five Constant Relations, but this is to be a new and special kind of extension. The Five Constant Relations were all between individuals. Liang's draws on the same quality of ethical relatedness, but this new relationship is to be between the individual, on the one side, and the whole community, on the other. (5) Community organization must emphasize connectedness to larger forms of organization, without which village autonomy alone cannot be effective or meet modern needs.

On these points Liang shares the sense of both Zhu Xi and Wang Yangming that new attempts at community organization must be based in past experience and build on earlier models—they must be rooted in the native social and cultural soil. Among those earlier Confucians who had written on the community compact and had seen it as a key to self-governance, Liang cites with approval the aforementioned seventeenth-century contemporary of Huang Zongxi, Lu Shiyi (1611–1672), a scholar in the Zhu Xi tradition whose critical reflections on problems of statecraft were included in Zhang Boxing's selective anthology of "orthodox" Neo-Confucian literature, the *Zhengyi-tang quanshu*.[13] Lu had emphasized local self-reliance and self-sufficiency in food, defense, and education by the coordination and mutual reinforcement of several cooperative communal organizations, including the community granary system *(shecang)*, the collective security system *(baojia)*, and community schools *(shexue)*, which generally had been operated, if at all, on a loose, largely uncoordinated basis. Like Huang Zongxi, he believed in the vital role of the educated Confucian scholar-official *(shi)* in government, but thought that these civil servants should gain practical experience along with their schooling by serving in the community compact on the local level. Thus they could bring this grassroots experience to bear on their conduct of office at the higher level.[14]

Lu's tripartite compact is an expanded version of Zhu Xi's, coordinating essential community services in education, agriculture, public works, and local defense with regular meetings of the whole community and a plural, cooperative leadership structure that is meant to bridge the gap between the people and the government *(guanfu)*. Lu invokes the passage from Confucius's *Analects* (12:7) in which the latter identifies public order as depending on three things: arms, food, and the confidence of the people, with the latter key to all else and arms the most dispensable of the three. On this basis Lu gives priority to education as the means for developing public morality and the shared values necessary to the workings of a consensual community *(yue)*, but like Mencius (as well as Hsü Heng and other earlier Neo-Confucians) he predicates this on a sound agricultural base, fortified in Lu's case by "ever-normal" granaries *(changping cang)* and charity granaries *(yicang)* that insure economic stability, and by public works that provide effective sharing of water resources. Community granaries, as cooperative institutions under local leadership to provide relief for poor farmers, had been advocated by Zhu Xi, endorsed by his colleague Lü Zuqian (1137–1181), and widely promoted by Zhu's early follower Zhen Dexiu (1178–1235), as well as by many later Zhu Xi schoolmen.[15]

It is significant, however, that Lu has to accept as customary the "village lecture" system identified with the founder of the Ming and spoken of by this time as the "lecture compact" *(jiangyue)*, and that he has to argue for attention to be paid in this process to the concerns of the common people. In contrast to the view that "public" *(gong)* is to be equated with "state" *(guan)*, Lu says that there should be discussion of "local public business," meaning by this that "the business of the people [*minshi*] is also public business [*gongshi*]," and that the discussion of these matters among the leadership of the several compact organizations should involve "the people of the whole community" *(i xiang zhi ren).*[16]

For Liang Shuming, the engagement of the community compact in these practical activities and discussion of people's actual needs would give substance to the functioning of the compact as more than an empty village ritual of moral indoctrination. In this he is prompted by his awareness of the superior group organization of the West and Japan, and goes beyond earlier Neo-Confucians like Zhu Xi, Wang Yangming, and Lu Shiyi, in recognizing the need for a larger civil infrastructure, as did Liang Qichao and other early twentieth-century reformers who likewise drew this conclusion from their observation of the West and Japan.[17] In the process, Liang Shuming also remedies a lack in Huang Zongxi's earlier Confucian constitutionalism, which provided for a kind of scholarly infrastructure in the schools as a restraint on the ruler's power, but did not deal with the problem on the same level as Liang's community compact. Though Huang spoke of "the people as masters," he was unable to articulate, as Liang Shuming did, an institutional means for active involvement of the people. Liang's sense of the need for organizational "connectedness" from the grassroots on up went beyond Huang in this respect, and suggested the groundwork for the kind of civil society China had previously lacked. On the other hand Liang seems not to have paid much attention to the state. Idealistic in this respect, and inclined towards a simplistic anarchism, he failed to address the realities of state power and the need for constitutional means to limit it, as Huang Zongxi and Liang Qichao had sought to do.

Liang Shuming was but one of many Chinese scholars and thinkers, whether within China or in exile abroad, who continued in Mao's time to speak for Confucian tradition. Several could be cited as upholding a Confucian alternative to either the radical individualisms attributed to the West at one extreme, or the conformity to party and state propagated by Liu Shaoqi at the other. What makes Liang of particular interest is that he, like some other Chinese of the pre-Mao era (that is, before the "liberation" that emancipated them from most of their personal freedoms), saw China's problem as not primarily one of state building or mass mobilization (as did Mao), but as one of rural reconstruction and reeducation.

Of the two cases cited here, the Communist Liu Shaoqi testifies, albeit inadvertently, to a Confucian personalism that he sees as dangerously individualistic, while Liang Shuming speaks for a Confucian communitarian tradition that somehow survives as a social ideal in spite of its past manhandling and persistent misappropriation by the state. Together these values bespeak a Confucian tradition that shares with the West a respect for the person that is in no way incompatible with human rights (and indeed is more amenable to these than are the dictates of an abusive state). Liang also shares a sense of the need for a genuine communitarianism that, in accord with the Confucian conception of rites, could be supportive of universal human rights as well. Together these complementary values belie any claim that modern human rights conceptions are exclusively Western, culture-bound, and inapplicable to China or the rest of Asia. They also belie any claim that communitarianism in China (or Asia) can be identified with the authoritarian state. On the contrary, the opposite is true: it is the state itself that has militated against Confucian communitarianism.

Exactly for this reason, however, the mere reassertion of Confucian personalism and communitarianism alone would not suffice to secure human rights. Though they might serve to create more autonomous, voluntary, and cooperative organizations on the local level, such community schools and community compacts, as the history of late Imperial China shows, could not survive or simply stand alone. Local autonomy and lateral networking do not in themselves serve the purposes of a civil infrastructure conveying public opinion and popular criticism upward to the top, where decisions are made on issues of national importance, often in a way prejudicial to the individual and community. Hence the constitutional structures advocated by Huang Zongxi and Liang Qichao still have relevance to the question of whether governance at the higher level is to be "by and of the people," rather than just "for the people" as the claim has been made by the Imperial dynasties and the one-party Dictatorship of the People's Democracy.

Today, with increased trade, economic development, and a growing middle class, many say that economic liberalization is bound to be followed by political liberalization. It is a fallacy, however, to assume that one need do no more about civil society and human rights than let ordinary economic developments take their course. Over the long term there may be some such effect, but it entails assumptions not warranted either by Chinese history or recent experience. At several stages of Chinese history commerce, industry, and a nascent middle class have grown to significant proportions, only to be hampered and stultified by state-imposed limitations. Again and again the Chinese have shown their entrepreneurial aptitude and skill whenever and wherever conditions allowed (and especially overseas, beyond the reach of Chinese rule), but in the long run of Chinese history these capacities have not thriven in the homeland. In other words, the continuing dominance of a centralized bureaucratic state in China has frustrated for centuries what Westerners tend to think of as a normal sequence of economic, social, and cultural development.

This suggests that, in the present situation, if Western businessmen recommend going slow on human rights and relying on economic development to do the job, a similar attitude on the part of Chinese businessmen may instead, as repeatedly in the past, lead to an accommodation with the state, a modus vivendi between businessmen and officials very similar to the limited bureaucratic capitalism of the later dynasties. This quite natural collusion is based on shared self-interest, with the state guaranteeing order and stability if not interfered with politically by the entrepreneurial class, and entrepreneurs profiting from the security and stability provided by the state. From this one gets a working alliance between businessmen (whether Chinese or foreign) and officialdom quite different from the bumptious, contentious middle-class politics that is presumed in the West to be the natural product of economic development.

There are already abundant signs of collusion and rampant corruption between business enterprise and opportunistic officials in a position to profit for themselves. Yet where is there any evidence of those doing business in or with China (whether Chinese, Japanese, or Western) actively interesting themselves in liberal democratic political movements? Moreover, seeing how this pattern of collusion and corruption between entrepreneurs and apparatchiks has become so widespread in former Communist countries elsewhere, one can hardly ignore it as a powerful factor complicating the prospects for liberal democracy.

It is true that there has been a significant movement recently to extend and improve legal protection for property and investment, and in general to regularize the conditions of trade in China. Since the 1970s, several American universities have joined in the promotion of Chinese legal studies to this end. It is also true that businessmen and others who suffer from official corruption and favoritism wish there could be greater legal and judicial protection against these. Still, despite some serious efforts along this line, there has been little success in curbing corruption. Most businessmen, Chinese or foreign, play the game themselves as best they can, making payoffs whenever it is to their own advantage, and wondering all the while when they may run afoul of an arbitrary and unpredictable judicial system. Thus a *Wall Street Journal* article of May 25, 1994, after a long recital of the woes of foreign businessmen in China, exposed to the vagaries of Chinese law, quotes one victim as saying, "I have a friend who does business here, who used to say, 'After China gets its economy going, that will eventually improve human rights.' Later this friend was arrested and detained himself. After his release he said, 'I was wrong before. First you have to improve human rights. Then you'll be able to improve the economy.'"

A striking illustration of the disparity between wishful thinking about economic and political liberalization and the realities of life in China is provided by two different headlines in the *New York Times* of May 25, 1995. One is the headline on Bill Bradley's op-ed piece, entitled: "Trade, the Engine of Democracy," a column in which he retrenched on his earlier strong assertion of the need to press for human rights in China, and instead optimistically proclaimed that expanding trade would, just by itself, inevitably pave the way to liberal democracy. In the business section of the same paper, the reality of the situation was exposed in an article headlined: "Between Marxism and the Market: A Chinese Manager Finds Corruption." The legacy of dynastic rule and Mao's Stalinist state is still a major fact of life in China. It is anything but a level playing field, since the apparatchiks use the power of entrenched position to alter radically the rules of the market game. This is in fact the practical meaning—or a good part of it—of what Deng and his successors have called "market so-cialism" or "the socialist market economy."

One might also consider another estimate of the prospects for liberal democracy from a *Wall Street Journal* correspondent, Marcus Brauchli, commenting on the idea that prosperity brings democracy. After discounting the seeming analogy between Taiwan (economic development leading to liberal democracy) and the mainland by pointing to the great disparity in income levels between the two, he adds:

> A bigger obstacle looms: Chinese with money—those who might be expected to demand more democracy—fear they would be victims, not beneficiaries, of a one-person, one-vote system. Some 250 million people in China's bustling cities and thriving coastal provinces are vastly better off now than they were a decade ago—but the other 900 million Chinese are peasants, eking out life in medieval-like conditions. Would the rich give control over their lives and destiny to these poor? . . .
>
> Thus, many of China's newly rich prefer the stability of the old system to the prospective turmoil of an electoral free-for-all. They have seen the turmoil that resulted from political liberalization in the former Soviet Union.[18]

One wonders if many businessmen, anywhere, would not come to the same conclusion. Have not those eager for trade with China and Vietnam been willing to forget about human rights and political democracy?

Underlying this situation, especially in China, is a still deeper crisis with the continuing sharp decline in public morality. This reflects, in turn, the almost total disillusionment with Marx-Leninism and Maoism, and the undermining of the earlier idealistic faith of Communist cadres, who had been indoctrinated to believe in dedicated "service to the people" only to find out that in practice this dedicated idealism was cynically manipulated by Mao, the Gang of Four, and others involved in power struggles at the top. Under Deng, everyone was told that there is nothing wrong in wanting to be rich, or in state enterprises (including the military) pursuing their own economic interests, even in developing their own deals abroad. No wonder then that competitive greed and corruption have come to dominate the scene, and while lip-service is still paid to the public interest and general welfare, in fact public morality continues seriously to decline.

Instead therefore of assuming that economic liberalization necessarily leads to political liberalization, the areas to watch are the educational sector and the communications media. The only signs of democratic life so far have appeared on university campuses. While individual businessmen may express liberal views, and dilate on how much better things have become since Deng's rule than they were under Mao's, the only evidences of democratic advocacy have come from scholarly and student quarters and even these efforts have been short-lived.

How to evaluate the actual potential of this glimmering democratic thought among intellectuals is a real problem. First of all, one must recognize that the university population is a tiny fraction of the total. Higher education is extremely limited in mainland China (in contrast to the much higher levels in Taiwan and the rest of East Asia). On the other hand, the state, its military arms, and its enterprises have a big stake in the training of experts to serve their own purposes, and this training cannot be wholly insulated from exposure to outside influences. Among the emigré scholars and graduate students from the People's Republic known to me, both refugees and others officially sponsored, it is clear that their thinking is affected by world trends, with the result of a serious erosion of belief in the official Marx-Leninist, Stalinist-Maoist ideology.[19]

Here again, however, it is sobering to consider the thinking of many Chinese today, often parallel to that of earlier Chinese, whose rational calculations of individual interest have not necessarily coincided with the public interest, as Liang Qichao and Liang Shuming themselves recognized. Instead their thinking often belies the expectation that the mere promotion of business and law together will produce a civil society, liberal democracy, and the affirmation of human rights in the near future. The case of a young educated Chinese woman, an escapee from the Tienanmen Square incident, illustrates both the poignance and pathos of the situation. As the daughter of Chinese academicians and someone trained in Chinese law, but now married to an American and working in New Jersey, she carries on a successful international legal business representing Americans in their dealings with the Chinese. She acknowledges that she "will never forget" the experience of "student-led democracy" at Tienanmen Square, but that now she "will avoid human rights and criminal law." . . . "When you've just graduated from college, especially after majoring in law, you want to get involved in politics . . . And you figure 'I can help my country.' . . . And then this happens [the crackdown at Tienanmen Square], and you feel like you are so small and you can't do anything to help . . . The government is so big, so powerful, that you better just forget about it. The way you can help is to live a good life, be a good person, do good things."[20]

This quite understandable conclusion (even arrived at in the comparative safety of the U.S.), is of course precisely what has worried generations of Confucians: how so often people, in the face of a government that is "so big, so powerful," could reconcile themselves to "being good" (for self and family) while forgetting about politics. The self-sacrificing ideal of the Sung dynasty Confucian statesman, Fan Zhongyan—"To be first in worrying about the world's worries and last in enjoying its pleasures"—is not to be found here.

For a more hopeful sign of the people's active concern with and participation in the political process, we can look back still further to a concept kept alive over the millennia, at least in the minds of those familiar with the Confucian classics, as recorded in the *Chronicle of Mr. Zuo (Zuo Zhuan)* more than two thousand years ago. It has to do with a popular revolt against the ruler of the state of Jin, and how this is seen as a natural consequence of the ruler's misrule. Interestingly these words are put in the mouth of a court musician advising his ruler:

> Shi Guang was attending the ruler of Jin. The latter said, "The people of Wei have driven out their ruler—what a terrible thing!"
>
> Shi Guang replied, "Perhaps it was the ruler himself who did terrible things. When a good ruler goes about rewarding good and punishing excess, he nourishes his people as though they were his children, shelters them like Heaven, accommodates them like the earth.
>
> "But if he exhausts the people's livelihood, deprives the spirits, skimps in the sacrifices to them and betrays the hopes of the populace, then he ceases to be the host of the nation's altars of the soil and grain, and what use is he? What can one do but expel him?
>
> "Heaven gave birth to the people and set up rulers to superintend and shepherd them and see to it that they do not lose their true nature as human beings. And because there are rulers, it provided helpers for them who would teach and protect them and see that they do not overstep the bounds. Hence the Son of Heaven has his chief officers, the feudal lords have their ministers, the ministers set up their collateral houses, gentlemen have their friends and companions, and the commoners, artisans, merchants, lackeys, shepherds and grooms all have their relatives and close associates who help and assist them. If one does good they praise him, if he errs they correct him, if he is in distress they rescue him, if he is lost they restore him.
>
> "Thus from the sovereign on down, each has his father or elder brother, his son or younger brother to assist and scrutinize his ways of management. The historians compile their documents, the blind musicians compose poems, the musicians chant admonitions and remonstrance, the high officials deliver words of correction, the gentlemen pass the word along, the commoners criticize, the merchants voice their opinions in the market and the hundred artisans contribute through their skills.

"Hence the 'Documents of Xia' says: 'The herald with his wooden-clappered bell goes about the roads, saying, "Let the officials and teachers correct the ruler, let the artisans pursue their skills and thereby offer remonstrance . . ."'

"Heaven's love for the people is very great. Would it then allow one man to preside over them in an arrogant and willful manner, indulging his excesses and casting aside the nature Heaven and earth allotted them? Surely it would not!"[21]

There is a parallel passage in another classic work, the *Discourses of the States (Guoyu)*, dealing with the tyranny of a King Li.[22] The attempt of one of his ministers to remonstrate with him ends on a similar note:

When the Son of Heaven listens to affairs of government, he causes his high ministers and others on down to the ranks of gentlemen to present poems, the blind musicians to present musical compositions, the historians to present their documents, the teachers to admonish, the pupil-less blind to recite, the dim-pupiled blind to chant, the hundred artisans to remonstrate, the commoners to pass along remarks, the close attendants of the ruler to offer unlimited correction, the ruler's parents and kin to assist and scrutinize, the blind musicians and historians to instruct and correct and the venerable elders to put these various admonitions into order. After that, the king examines and applies them. In this way, affairs can be carried out without miscarriage.[23]

I cite these two passages from early Confucian literature (which should no doubt be taken as prescriptive more than descriptive accounts) to illustrate two points. One is that both in early China and in later Imperial China the Confucians emphasized the benefits of free political discussion and open criticism of those in power. Particularly noteworthy is the Zuo Commentary's [*Zuo Zhuan's*] characterization of this function as being carried out on all levels of society, including commoners as well as clearly handicapped and disadvantaged persons. One might note at the same time that it is primarily the educated Confucian elite who were said to have taken the active responsibility for this in government, and especially in the schools.

This is not democracy, but it allows for elements of free speech and assembly and provides some glimmerings of how a civil society was conceived in China. Other cases could be cited in Chinese history that give evidence of a liberal Confucian tradition supportive of and protective of certain humane values, especially in education, in schools, and in ruling councils, but usually defined in terms of consensual rites, not legal compulsion.

As this tradition becomes more fully studied and understood, it will show that values supportive of human rights are not lacking in Confucian tradition, and that there are multicultural grounds for thinking of these rights as more broadly "human" than just Western. It will also give the lie to any contention that individual human rights are foreign to China, whether such assertions come from those within China who wish to exclude these rights as dangerous foreign objects landing in China, or from those in the West who consider human rights to be peculiarly Western conceptions virtually untransplantable to alien and inhospitable Chinese soil. A recent development even in the West, human rights should not be seen as fixed in one form only, but as seeds planted and growing from roots in different cultural soils. If they are to thrive, it cannot be through a monoculture, but through a multicultural dialogue, aiming at a better mutual understanding of shared human values.

Conclusion

The original construction of the Universal Declaration of Human Rights involved the participation of Confucians, and gained the subsequent adherence to it of countries sharing Confucian cultures. There is thus no basis for asserting any inherent incompatibility between Confucianism and the human rights to which most nations subscribe.

The person as understood by Confucianism in the context of human relationships is no less entitled to respect than the individual in Western human rights concepts. Thus the dichotomy of "individual" versus "community" rights is inapplicable and misleading in this case.

At the same time, Confucianism emphasizes particular forms of human respect, personal responsibility, and mutual support that could supplement modern legalistic definitions of human rights and help us to deal with social problems that do not yield to legal solutions alone. To learn from the experience of the Confucians—in East Asia as a whole, and not just China—need not mean surrendering anything of individual rights to the community or state, but only gaining a deeper awareness of human interdependence and social sensibilities.

This is not to say that the Confucian record in human relations has always been exemplary. Indeed in the matter of women's rights, it is questionable whether the treatment of women in China, as accepted or tolerated among many Confucians, met even the Confucians' own standards of humaneness, reciprocity, rightness, and equity, let alone those of the modern West.

Although traditional China was not without semi-autonomous organizations on the local level, especially family-type institutions relatively effective in dealing with local needs, it had difficulty in developing a civil infrastructure by which to bridge the gap between local organization and a strong, centralized, authoritarian state. Without adequate channels of communication from the lower level to the higher, and without enough of the population educated and informed sufficiently to participate in the discussion of public policy, it has been difficult to curb the abuse of power, or to assert and defend—much less to advance—people's rights and human rights.

Authentic Confucian spokesmen from at least the eleventh century onwards recognized the need for community organization in the form of community schools and community compacts (including community granaries). However limited was their success in establishing and maintaining these, the need for such was kept alive by the active advocacy of Confucian scholar-officials. Other Confucians called for schools and academies as centers of public discussion, and for a constitutional order providing for wider participation in the political process. Thus, although the Confucian communitarian tradition has been overshadowed by state power and bureaucratism, it did continue to propose, albeit in adverse circumstances, consensual alternatives for promoting a more balanced relationship among the individual, the community, and the state. It is to such Confucian advocates, and not spokesmen for state power, that one should look for a genuine Chinese communitarianism as the basis for the advancement of human rights.

Without such advocacy, one cannot expect economic development and rising affluence alone to produce a civil society or constitutional order protective of human rights.

Where such advocacy is repressed today, it is not unreasonable, and indeed becomes most necessary, for others to join in a dialogue on human rights that is open to all comers and open to the discussion of all issues—in East or West. Although this dialogue should be multicultural—respectful of the different ways in which diverse traditions express their human concerns—these concerns are no longer just local or national; they are global in scope and everybody's business. The responsibility for them falls most directly on those in authority, who cannot claim them to be exclusively matters of domestic concern and responsibility. Today the urgency of worldwide environmental and security problems that cannot be cordoned off nationally compels us to adopt a common approach and common standards to these inseparable problems of the human–earth community.

Afterword

Fifteen years ago, in lectures at the Chinese University of Hong Kong dedicated to the eminent Chinese historian Ch'ien Mu (Qian Mu), I presented my views on aspects of the Confucian tradition, which I entitled *The Liberal Tradition in China*. There was, I realized at the time, some risk of misunderstanding if I applied a term with such strong Western connotations (even before it became stigmatized as the "L" word) to a tradition generally thought of only as conservative (if not indeed wholly reactionary and repressive). Nonetheless it seemed worth the risk of some misunderstanding for me to draw attention to important elements in Confucian tradition hitherto ignored because they did not fit the accepted stereotype.

Somewhat the same is true of my use in this book of such terms as "individualism," "personalism," "communitarianism," and "constitutionalism," which have their own meanings in the West and are usually thought improbable as aspects of a tradition defined by some, almost from the start, as totally "other." Confucianism is in some ways "other," but how much so depends on one's looking only for historical and cultural differences and not for human commonalities.

One reason for my willingness to risk some misunderstanding in my use of the word "liberal" was that already, in the seventies, China had become an issue in the discussions of the human rights program at Columbia and elsewhere. At that time some people in the West were quite ready to dismiss China as off limits to human rights. In this view the Chinese and other Asian peoples had been so long inured to repression and so lacking in any sense of individual human dignity that concepts of human rights were essentially foreign to them. This thought then became father to two almost equally dangerous attitudes: that one can dismiss human rights as meaningless or inapplicable to people outside the Western tradition—which probably means writing off a large portion of the human race as beyond the range of our active sympathy; or alternatively that, accepting them as benighted, only half-civilized folk, it will be for the West to assume a great civilizing mission in bringing to them the gospel of human rights. By the recipients, however, such condescension was sure to be perceived, or at least portrayed, as arrogant and self-righteous, so that such help as we might have given to persons actually suffering the deprivation of human rights would easily be discredited by those wishing to persist in their denial.

This was no imagined specter. The view that Western liberal values and democratic institutions are intrinsically alien or artificial—"undesirable formalisms," as Liu Shaoqi once described them—has been exploited by authoritarians of both the left and right in Asia. And the dangers from such a misconception—from a failure to analyze with sufficient care the similarities and differences in the varied cultural and social expressions of these values—were likely to be compounded by a new development on the East Asian scene; the rehabilitation of Confucianism as an important factor in the ethos of East Asian peoples and their undoubted, even if somewhat belated, success in achieving economic miracles in the latter half of the twentieth century. Where Confucianism not so long ago had been berated as an obstacle to progress, it was now being called the key to the disciplined work ethic of the East Asians, to their acceptance of authority and paternalistic organization as the basis for more efficient economic enterprise, and to a political stability conducive to industrial growth and productivity. Originally a misconception of doctrinaire "liberals," the image of Confucianism as essentially authoritarian and conservative was now falling into the hands of others who had their own interests and illiberal purposes to promote.

To be sure one could not let such considerations dominate scholarly inquiry, but what greater scholarly virtue, one might still ask, attached to the presumption that the Confucian tradition is inherently conservative rather than interwoven of both conservative and liberal strands? Given that such terms had become the common currency of political discourse, no one, to my knowledge, had questioned Mary Wright's right to talk about "The Last Stand of Chinese Conservatism,"[1] even though she took no great pains to define her terms. And if we simply left it at that, without considering the possible presence of liberal elements in the same tradition, were we not tacitly accepting a double standard of criticism?

I could appreciate the feeling that, for analytic purposes, there must be some mean between definitions of "liberal" or "liberalism" that were either too narrow and Western-centered or so broad as to include any kind of reformism. I also shared some people's misgivings over a conception so loose as to leave unspecified what many would feel were indispensable ingredients of liberalism—whether as basic principles or institutions. On the other hand, I felt equally the need to keep one's conception open enough so that one could accept non-Western formulations of these values, in the past or future, which are not culture-bound. Thus, in *The Liberal Tradition in China* I employed as "working definitions" characterizations of liberalism by Morris Cohen, Charles Frankel, and Gilbert Murray that at least could not be disqualified as contaminated by the suspected prejudices of Orientalists, though they might be limited by other Occidental preconceptions. While believing that each shed some light on the problem, and that each contributed something to our understanding of what liberalism has been and could be, I resisted the demand for a fixed and final definition to be applied invariably to all phenomena one might so investigate.

Short of that, as my own "working definition," I am willing to put forward what constitutes for me the essence of the liberal attitude or approach, trying to identify certain core values even while necessarily leaving others open to interpretation.

First, I would say that any long-term view of liberalism must presuppose a positive commitment to humane values—such as the value of human life and the dignity of the human person—however these may be identifiable in different social and cultural traditions. Shared human values—and "Asian values" no less than others—are irreducibly marked by elements of both commonality and diversity. As Mark Van Doren wisely said in his *Liberal Education,* long before the outbreak of the so-called "culture wars,"

> Imagination always has work to do, whether in single minds or in the general will . . . Without it, for instance, the West can come to no conclusions about the East which war and fate are rapidly making a necessary object of its knowledge. Statistics and surveys of the East will not produce what an image can produce: an image of difference, so that no gross offenses are committed against the human fact of strangeness, and an image of similarity, even of identity, so that nothing homely is forgotten.[2]

This simultaneous affirmation of similarity and difference—the positive commitment to shared human values in the midst of cultural diversity—may run somewhat counter to a prevalent modern view of liberalism as bound up almost exclusively with a skeptical or critical habit of mind, which often dwells on differences at the expense of commonalities. To me the critical approach is the second essential element, but not the first. There must be affirmative belief and commitment before doubt and skepticism come into play. A "critical temper" that is content simply to debunk and deconstruct does no credit to human intelligence. It is essentially parasitic and eventually sterile.

Nevertheless the cultivated habit of distancing oneself from received opinion, suspending judgment, and reflecting upon one's own beliefs and conduct is certainly the next most important element in a liberal view of things. A third follows directly from the first and second: that one must be ready to entertain opposing views and engage them in open discourse, on terms as nearly as possible equal with others. This process has often been described as "the free marketplace of ideas," but in a world that is getting smaller and more crowded, with the marketplace generally much less free and often less than fair, one is compelled to think of other political and social arrangements that could sustain this open discourse. Thus, lastly, institutional frameworks, legal enactments, and countervailing power structures, protective of this open exchange of information and opinion, become all the more critical to the survival of any kind of liberalism.

This is a brief and obviously minimal account of essential liberal principles. It attempts to identify the core rather than the totality of liberalism. And it is not meant to suggest that "liberal" or "liberalism" are ultimate values. Left out of consideration are many of the religious, political, economic, and social factors that would affect the outcome in any given set of historical circumstances. But I think these are basic criteria that can be applied to liberal learning, liberal education, and liberal politics anywhere. Anyone who accepted them as indispensable to his conception of "liberal" would, I believe, be able to recognize their counterpart values in the Confucian tradition, though not without some qualification in each case and perhaps with the greatest reservation made, in China, concerning the last of the four: the institutional infrastructure and countervailing forces that I have spoken of here as a civil society. This last question I have addressed in certain of its aspects in *The Trouble with Confucianism* (Harvard University Press, 1991). Without going further into the matter here, I bring it to the attention of any reader who might draw from the present book the notion—I hope unwarranted and certainly unintended—that Confucianism, just in itself, was a liberal tradition capable of generating and sustaining human rights without the benefit of converging trends and influences from outside the culture.

Still, if there has been one aspect of Confucian tradition most seriously underestimated in the West, it has been its capacity for self-criticism and self-renewal. In this book I have given examples of this continuity, reflection, and redevelopment in the case of Confucian thinking about education and community organization, from classic sources like Mencius and the books of Rites through Zhu Xi, Xu Heng, Wang Yang-ming, and other major scholar officials of the Ming and Qing periods down into modern times. The fact that they had limited success in translating their ideas into mainstream institutions is no more reason to dismiss them than is the similar fate of much liberal, communitarian, and socialist thinking in the West. Nor should it be forgotten that many of these ideas were powerful and influential enough to become institutionalized in Korea (though that is a separate story).[3]

Failure to read the Confucian record itself as a continuing discourse of internal self-criticism has also meant a failure to recognize how Western influences, instead of being wholly at odds with Chinese tradition, could operate to reinforce liberal tendencies already at work in this traditional discourse, even though the latter were not politically dominant. One effect has been to heighten the impression, in the minds of some, that needed changes could only come about through all-out Westernization (even at the cost of revolutionary upheaval), and in the minds of others, defensive of tradition, that Western liberal influences had to be resisted as fundamentally inimical to traditional culture.

When I first broached these ideas about liberal elements in the Chinese tradition, the future of Confucianism was much in doubt. In the midst of the Cultural Revolution the institutions that had been the main carriers of Confucian culture no longer served that purpose. The family system was under severe attack. The school system, once a stronghold of Confucian learning, had long since been Westernized; and after 1949 the scriptures of Marx, Lenin, Stalin, and Mao had replaced the Confucian canon. Even today the serious study of Confucianism lags, and it still has little place in the educational curriculum of the People's Republic.

Meanwhile official sponsorship and semi-official promotion of a conservative brand of Confucianism has become a virtual growth industry, now even of multinational proportions in East and Southeast Asia. Whether this can be considered a genuine revival is of course open to question, but it can hardly be doubted that Confucianism (or what goes for it), and not any form of Marx-Leninism, has become the claimed ideological justification for one-party rule, for openly rejecting "peaceful evolution" to democracy, and for suppressing demonstrations such as those at Tiananmen Square in May–June 1989.

When young people demonstrated at Tiananmen Square, they were using the means of political expression best known to them in history: sporadic student scholarly protests at the Han and Sung imperial courts, the same in the nationalist protest movement of May 4th, 1919 (part of the revolutionary movement that had entered into Communist "history") and the Cultural Revolution of the 1960s and early 1970s. By this time (1989) the Democracy Wall and its "Big Character" posters had been taken away, and young people fell back on the only kind of political activism most of their generation had seen or heard about, typified by the marching Red Guards in the Cultural Revolution.

Where the Red Guards had not hesitated to use force, however, the Tiananmen demonstrators were notably non-violent. Admittedly, stomping and shouting in a public square is not the best way to resolve political differences, but in the absence of any other due process—such as the kind of civil infrastructure discussed in this book—what recourse did people have? Idealistic and enthusiastic, but politically inexperienced, poorly organized, and improvising from day to day, the demonstrators easily let their peaceful intentions and genuinely patriotic protests get out of hand—over-extending the capabilities of their own haphazard leadership to judge what one could reasonably expect to achieve in that chaotic situation.

Nor is it difficult to understand why Deng Xiaoping reacted as he did to the Tiananmen Square situation. Not only as a general in the war of revolution, but as a survivor of the internecine warfare of the Cultural Revolution, he had shown himself to be a decisive and resolute leader. What happened at Tiananmen Square—and it was truly a "happening," not a plot or conspiracy of any kind—struck him as threatening to bring on the same governmental paralysis and anarchy to which Cultural Revolution had led. Deng had joined with the Army in suppressing that earlier disorder, and it is not surprising that, in a moment of intense crisis, he would reach for the same military means of dealing with the danger of anarchy so similar to that precipitated by the Cultural Revolution.

Nevertheless, if the Communist Party has claimed for itself the exclusive right of political leadership and educational authority, it must accept responsibility for what happened. Mao himself and the Party along with him had encouraged political activism in the 1960s and early 1970s; now it provided no outlets through which young people could express themselves politically—no ordered process by which they could gain practical experience, acquire greater maturity of political judgment, and fulfill their aspirations. For the Party instead to make accusations of conspiracy and treason against the demonstrators when it, as sole wielder of educational power and authority for forty years, should have borne the responsibility for their frustration and immaturity, was to forfeit any claim it might have had to moral legitimacy.

It is a fair question now whether Deng's successors do not share the same responsibility as he. To that question my own answer, as a concerned outsider, reflects my personal experience in having met three times with Jiang Zemin, the current president of the People's Republic and general secretary of the Party. One of these occasions, in 1994, does not really count; it was for Jiang simply a photo opportunity at the Great Hall of the People when he asked me to stand next to him for publicity purposes, and nothing but the usual pleasantries were exchanged. The other two occasions were with small scholarly delegations, one for a half hour, the other for almost two hours. Such limited acquaintance does not confer on one any special authority, but for what it is worth my impression of Jiang was of a person open and forthcoming, no more guarded and discreet than one would expect of someone in his position; he was intelligent, moderate, forward-looking in his views and not at all ideologically doctrinaire (for whatever that kind of pragmatism may be worth in politically volatile and highly pressured situations).

(Parenthetically, when I reported these impressions to "professional" China-watchers and Pekingologists later, the latter easily dismissed them, quite convinced that Jiang was only a transitional figure; he would be gone soon, they said, like [General Secretary] Hua Guofeng after Mao's death. That was 1989; as of 1998, Jiang is still there and, if anything, in an even stronger position.)

Whatever Deng had in mind when he chose Jiang as his successor, one has to assume that he expected Jiang not only to carry forward his economic program, but also to complete unfinished political business. Hardline voices in Beijing insist that this cannot mean "peaceful evolution" to liberal democracy, and their very insistence confirms that such a development could not just happen without some necessary struggle. One can only hope that others, if not Jiang himself, will join in making that effort to democratize, that it will come about peacefully, and that the outcome, if not wholly to the tastes of foreign observers, will serve to some degree the aspirations that the younger generation tried to express at Tiananmen.

The measure of their success, however, will not be seen in how often they invoke "Asian values," Confucian pieties, or communitarian ideals that merely mask the perpetuation of a powerful state apparatus, but in how they help to build, in due time and process, a political and social infrastructure that meets the standards of both Western and Confucian civility, provides for an independent legal system protective of the rights of both the individual and the group, and preserves those elements of Chinese tradition that can still nurture the dignity of the Confucian person.

Notes

1. *"Asian Values" and Confucianism*

1. Howard French, "Africa Looks East for a New Model." *New York Times*, February 4, 1996, 4:1.

2. *Mencius*, 4b:14.

3. Wm. Theodore de Bary, ed., *The Unfolding of Neo-Confucianism* (New York: Columbia University Press, 1975), p. 32.

4. Sumner Twiss and Tu Weiming, in Wm. Theodore de Bary and Tu Weiming, eds., *Confucianism and Human Rights* (New York: Columbia University Press, 1997), pp. 44, 322–329.

5. Amartya Sen, "Asian Values and Human Rights." Hans Morgenthau Memorial Lecture, Carnegie Council on Ethics and International Affairs, New York, May 1, 1997. Published in *The New Republic*, July 14, 1997, pp. 33–40.

2. *Individualism and Personhood*

1. *Analects* 2:7; 17:21.

2. Ron Guey Chu, "Rites and Rights in Ming China." Paper presented to the Conference on Confucianism and Human Rights, East-West Center, Honolulu, August 14–17, 1995.

3. *Analects* 2:4.

4. Thomas Berry provides a broad conspectus of Western and Chinese views of the individual and person, bringing out both their contrasting and complimentary features, in his "Individualism and Wholism in Chinese Tradition: The Religious Cultural Context," a paper prepared for an ACLS/NEH-sponsored conference, "Individualism and Holism in Chinese Thought," held at the Breckinridge Center in York, Maine, June 24–29, 1981.

5. Anthony C. Yu, "Altered Accents: A Comparative View of Liberal

Education." Remarks delivered at the fortieth anniversary of Hong Kong Baptist University, April 17, 1996. In *Criterion* 35:2 (Spring/Summer 1996), Divinity School of the University of Chicago, p. 10.

6. *Analects* 2:20.

7. *Analects* 18:6.

8. Liji, yueji 1; Legge, *Li chi,* reprint (New York: University Books, New Hyde Park, 1967), vol. II, p. 97.

9. Burton Watson, trans., *Hsün tzu: Basic Writings* (New York: Columbia University Press, 1962), p. 89.

10. As shown by the later examples of Huang Zongxi and Lü Liuliang, discussed in chapters 3 and 6.

3. Laws and Rites

1. *Mencius* 3A:3, translation by Irene Bloom in Wm. Theodore de Bary et al., eds., *Sources of Chinese Tradition,* 2nd ed. (New York: Columbia University Press, 1998).

2. *Sishu jiangyi,* 1686 ed., 29:10ab, on *Zhongyong* 32; translated in Wm. Theodore de Bary, *Learning for One's Self* (New York: Columbia University Press, 1991), p. 326.

3. *Sishu jiangyi,* 37:1b–2a, on *Mengzi* 4B:3; *Yulu,* 40:2ab; Wm. Theodore de Bary, *Learning for One's Self: Essays on the Individual in Neo-Confucian Thought* (New York: Columbia University Press, 1991), p. 329.

4. As quoted in Irene Bloom et al., eds., *Religious Diversity and Human Rights* (New York: Columbia University Press, 1996), p. 139.

5. Zhang Boxing, *Zhengyi tang quanshu,* Siku quanshu zhenben ed., vol. 724, chs. 11, 12.

6. de Bary et al., eds., *Sources of Chinese Tradition,* pp. 154–155.

4. School and Community

1. *Analects* 13:23.

2. *Miao xue dianli* (Siku quanshu zhenben ed.) 6:22a–24a Cheng zong shili xiaoxue shushu; Yu Ji, "Jingshi dadian xulu," in Su Tianjue, *Guochao wenlei,* Sibu congkan ed. 40:17a, 41:6ab (also in Wenyuan ge Siku quanshu ed., vol. 1367, pp. 499, 509). Charles O. Hucker, *A Dictionary of Official Titles in Imperial China* (Stanford: Stanford University Press, 1985), no. 2789.

3. *Sishu jiangyi,* 1686 ed., 37:1b–2a; *Sishu yülu,* Tiankailou 1684 ed., 40:2ab.

4. *Jiao min bangwen,* in *Huang Ming zhishu,* vol. 3, pp. 1433–1434, as translated by Edward Farmer for the second edition of *Sources of Chinese Tradition,* edited by Wm. Theodore de Bary et al. (New York: Columbia University Press, 1998).

5. Chen Xianzhang, in *Chen Baishaji.* Wenyuange Siku quanshu 1246/19–20 (1:24b–25a) Chengxiang xien shexueji; Wang Yangming, in *Wang Wencheng gong quanshu,* Wen yuange Siku quanshu ed. 1265/485, 17:51b Xingju shexuebei, and 1265/489 (17:60b–61a) Banxing shexue jiaotiao; Li Mengyang, *Kongtongji,* Siku quanshu zhenben vol. 8, 42:9a–11b Nanxin er xien zaicheng shexuebei. I have benefited here from the extensive researches (some unpublished) of Dr. Ron Guey Chu, Academia Sinica, Taipei.

6. Ho Ping-ti, *The Ladder of Success in Imperial China* (New York: Columbia University Press, 1962), pp. 195–196.

7. Angela Ki-che Leung, "Elementary Education in the Lower Yangtze Region in the Seventeenth and Eighteenth Centuries," in Benjamin Elman and Alexander Woodside, *Education and Society in Late Imperial China, 1600–1900* (Berkeley: University of California Press, 1994), p. 382.

8. Angela Leung, "Elementary Education," p. 385 quoting Huang Luchong in 1699.

9. William T. Rowe, "Education and Empire in Southwest China," in Elman and Woodside, *Education and Society in Late Imperial China,* p. 428.

10. Evelyn Rawski, "Economic and Social Foundations," in David Johnson, Andrew Nathan, and Evelyn Rawski, eds., *Popular Culture in Late Imperial China* (Berkeley: University of California Press, 1986), p. 11.

11. See my *Self and Society in Ming Thought* (New York: Columbia University Press, 1970), pp. 1–27, 145–249.

12. Adapted from translation by Joanna Handlin Smith for the second edition of de Bary et al., eds., *Sources of Chinese Tradition,* ch. 24D.

13. Adapted from the translations of William Rowe for the second edition of de Bary et al., eds., *Sources of Chinese Tradition,* ch. 28A.

14. See my *Liberal Tradition in China* (Hong Kong: Chinese University Press of Hong Kong, 1983), pp. 37–38.

15. Thomas H. C. Lee, "Academies: Official Sponsorship and Sup-

pression," in Frederic Landauer and Huang Chun-chieh, *Imperial Rulership and Cultural Change in Imperial China* (Seattle: University of Washington Press, 1994), pp. 135–138.

16. Benjamin Elman, *Classicism, Politics and Kinship* (Berkeley: University of California Press, 1990), pp. 25–31, 322–323; and Kai-wing Chow, *The Rise of Confucian Ritualism in Late Imperial China* (Stanford: Stanford University Press, 1994), pp. 224–225. See also Angela Leung, "Elementary Education," pp. 388, 401–403.

17. Ron Guey Chu, "Scholarly Autonomy and Political Dissent in Local Academies of the Early Ch'ing," in *Chung-kuo wen-chih yen-chiu chi k'an* (Taipei: Academia Sinica 3, March 1993), pp. 629, 633.

18. Rowe, "Education and Empire," p. 427.

19. Statecraft thinkers like Wei Yuan (1794–1856) in the early nineteenth century registered the need for basic reform, carrying on the tradition of early Qing reformism by Huang Zongxi, Gu Yanwu, Lu Sheyi, and others, but they lacked the political support needed to make their advocacy effective. See the translations of Philip Kuhn and Liu Kuang-ching for chapter 28 of the second edition of de Bary et al., eds., *Sources of Chinese Tradition.*

20. See Barry Keenan, "Diary Pedagogy in Lower Yangtze Academies 1830–1900," paper presented to Yuelu Academy Conference on "Confucianism and Education," Changsha, China, August 25–28, 1996.

21. Elman, Classicism, Politics, and Kinship, pp. 304–305; James Polachek, "Literati Groups and Group Politics in Nineteenth Century China" (Ph.D. diss., University of California, 1977).

5. The Community Compact

1. Wm. Theodore de Bary, *The Liberal Tradition in China* (Hong Kong: The Chinese University Press, 1983; New York: Columbia University Press, 1983).

2. In *Reflections on Things at Hand (Jinsi lu)*, Zhu also quoted Cheng Yi's account of Cheng Hao's attempts to reform local administration by a program of moral self-reform and mutual aid led by scholar-officials. See Wing-tsit Chan, trans., Chu Hsi and Lu Tsu-chien, comp., *Reflections on Things at Hand* (New York: Columbia University Press, 1967), p. 225.

3. de Bary, *Liberal Tradition*, pp. 32–34.

4. Robert Hymes, "Academies and the Local Community," in Wm.

Theodore de Bary and J. Chaffee, eds., *Neo-Confucian Education* (Berkeley: University of California Press, 1989), pp. 440–444.

5. Monika Ubelhör, "The Community Compact in the Sung," in de Bary and Chaffee, eds., *Neo-Confucian Education,* pp. 380–381. In view of the strong emphasis put by other writers on the "statist" character of the *Rites* [or Offices] *of Zhou* (*Zhouli* or *Zhouguan*), the distinction Ubelhör draws here between the voluntaristic, communitarian character of the Lü compact and the more hierarchical scheme of the *Rites of Zhou* is noteworthy.

6. Ibid., p. 382.

7. Ibid., p. 386.

8. Ibid., pp. 386–387.

9. *Zhu zi daquan,* Sibu beiyao ed. 100:6a.

10. Ubelhör, "The Community Compact in the Sung," p. 388.

11. de Bary, *Liberal Tradition,* p. 65.

12. Chung-li Chang, *The Chinese Gentry* (Seattle: University of Washington Press, 1955), p. 65.

13. Ibid.

14. Ibid., pp. 199–200.

15. Victor Mair, "Language and Ideology in the Written Popularization of the Sacred Edict," in David Johnson, Andrew Nathan, and Evelyn Rawski, eds., *Popular Culture in Late Imperial China* (Berkeley: University of California Press, 1985), pp. 325–359.

16. Ibid., pp. 325–326.

17. Ibid., pp. 329–349; Edward L. Farmer, "Social Legislation of the First Ming Emperor: Orthodoxy as a Foundation of Authority," in Kwang-ching Liu, ed., *Orthodoxy in Late Imperial China* (Berkeley: University of California Press, 1990), pp. 111–125.

18. See Mair, "Language and Ideology," pp. 329, 331, 340–342, 349, 359.

19. Ibid., pp. 335, 354, 355.

20. Ibid., pp. 335, 351, 352.

21. See Li Laizhang, *Li Shanyuan quanji,* 1:1ab "Shengyou xuanjiangyi zhu."

22. Mair, "Language and Ideology," pp. 344–345.

23. Ibid., pp. 332, 340, 342, 345, 346, 348.

24. Ibid., pp. 341–342.

25. Ibid., pp. 353–354.

26. Ibid., p. 350.

27. Ibid., p. 347, n63; pp. 354, 357. Hereafter page references to this source appear as interlinear notes in the text.

28. *Zhu zi daquan* (Sibu beiyao ed.) 100:5b–6a.

29. *Zhu zi daquan* 100:5ab. Translation adapted from Ron Guey Chu in de Bary and Chaffee, eds., *Neo-Confucian Education*, p. 262.

30. *Zhu zi daquan* 99:1b–2a. Trans. adapted from Ron Guey Chu in de Bary and Chaffee, eds., *Neo-Confucian Education*, p. 264.

31. Übelhör, "The Community Compact in the Sung," p. 377.

32. Evidence found in the *Popular Encyclopedia for Daily Use (Riyong leishu)* and in particular the *Wanyong zhengzong* preserved in the Hōsa Bunko, Nagoya, as reported by Sakai Tadao in "Yi Yulgok and the Community Compact," in Wm. Theodore de Bary and Ja-Hyun Kim Haboush, eds., *The Rise of Neo-Confucianism in Korea* (New York: Columbia University Press, 1985), p. 325.

33. See Edward L. Farmer, "Social Order in Early Ming China," in Brian McKnight, ed., *Law and the State in Traditional East Asia* (Honolulu: University of Hawaii Press, 1987), pp. 14, 20–22.

34. See Anita M. Andrew, "The Local Community in Early Ming Social Legislation: Ming Taizu's Approach to Transformation and Control in the 'Great Warning.'" *Ming Studies* 20 (Spring 1985), pp. 57–68.

35. Jiaomin bangwen, as contained in *Huang Ming zhishu*, ch. 9 (Taipei: Cheng-wen, 1969), vol. 3, pp. 1419–1420. See also George Jer-lang Chang, "The Placard of People's Instructions." *Ming Studies* 7 (Fall 1978), pp. 63–72.

36. As noted in the preceding chapter the actual institution of the *she-hsüeh* in the Yüan appears to have been done in 1270 by Zhang Wenqian (1217–1282), a close associate of Xu Heng, following Xu's earlier memorial to Khubilai in 1266 and Zhang's appointment as minister of the Court of Agriculture *(sinong si qing)* in 1270. There is a strong similarity of language among the successive expositions of Mencius, Zhu Xi, Xu Heng, Zhang Wenqian, and finally Ming Taizu's decree of 1375 "reestablishing" the *she xue*. See Mencius 1A:7(24); Zhu Xi, *Daxue zhang zhu* (Taipei: Zhongguo zixue mingju jicheng ed.), 1:1; *Meng zi ji zhu* 1:15–16, pp. 486–487; Xu Heng, "Shiwu wushi," in *Luzhai quanshu* (Chūbun, Kindai kanseki sōkan ed.), 3:161 ff. esp. 186–189; *Miao xue dianli* (Siku quanshu zhenben ed.), 6:22a–24a Cheng zong shili xiaoxue shushu; You Ji, "Jingshi dadian xulu," in Su Tianjue, *Guochao wenlei*, Sibu congkan ed. 40:17a, 41:6ab (also in Wenyuan ge SKQS ed., vol. 1367, pp. 499, 509); *Ming Taizu shilu* (Jiangsu guoxue tushuguan

ed.), 96:4b, Hongwu 8 year, 1st mo., dinghai (February 27, 1375); *Xu wenxian tongkao* (Shanghai: Commercial Press *Shi tong* ed., 1936), 50:3244b. For the locus classicus of the village school see *Liji* (Maiwang xian guan ed. of *Shisanjing zhusu*), 36:2a Hsüeh-chi. I am grateful to Professor Yan-shuan Lao for pointing out the role of Zhang Wenqian in this continuing process.

37. See Song Lian, *Song xueshi wenji* [SBCK ed.] 75:1ab; Wm. Theodore de Bary, *Neo-Confucian Orthodoxy and the Learning of the Mind-and-Heart* (New York: Columbia University Press, 1981), pp. 153–154, 157–158.

38. Yu Ji, *Jingshi dadian xulu*, in Su Tianjue, comp., *Guochao [Yüan] wenlei* 40:17a Fu-tian, nongsang (also in Wenyuange Siku quanshu ed., vol. 1367, p. 509) and 41:6a–7a Li dian, xuexiao.

39. John W. Dardess, *Confucianism and Autocracy* (Berkeley: University of California Press, 1983), pp. 215–216.

40. See Leif Littrup, *Sub-Bureaucratic Government in Ming Times* (Oslo: Universitets Forleget, 1981), pp. 58–59; Farmer, "Social Order," pp. 11–14, 18; George Jer-lang Chang, "The Village Elder System of the Early Ming" in *Ming Studies* 7 (Fall 1978), pp. 53–55. It is known that a recommendation was made to establish a system of community compacts in the early Ming (Hongwu period?) but nothing came of it. See Ubelhör, "The Community Compact in the Sung," p. 388. Apparently Taizu thought the arrangements made in his "Jiaomin bangwen" served this purpose.

41. "Jiaomin bangwen," pp. 1405–1406; cp. Chang, p. 63.

42. See Kimura Eiichi, "'Sitte' to Shushi no gaku" in *Chūgoku tetsugaku no tankyū* (Tokyo: Sōbunsha, 1981), pp. 279–296; and Sakai Tadao, *Chūgoku zensho no kenkyū* (Tokyo: Kobundō, 1960), p. 39.

43. See for instance his essays on popular customs, and the promotion of agriculture addressed to local audiences, in his *Shi zuwen, Zhu zi daquan* (Sibu beiyao ed.) 99:5b, and Quan nongwen, ibid., 8a–9a. This does not mean that *Zhong* ("loyalty," "fidelity," "being true") was not important for Zhu Xi in other contexts, but only that it was not emphasized by Zhu in his formulation of a communitarian ethic.

44. See his Bailudong shuyuan jieshi in *Zhuzi daquan* 74:16b–17a; and de Bary, *The Liberal Tradition*, p. 35.

45. See Kimura, "Sitte," pp. 288–289. It should be noted that Zhu did not give the same high priority to the so-called *Classic of Filial Piety* as he did to the virtue itself. Among classics to be read he accorded the *Xiao Jing* no prominent place.

46. Littrup, *Sub-Bureaucratic Government*, p. 60.

47. Sakai, *Zensho,* pp. 41–42; Ubelhör, "The Community Compact in the Sung," pp. 387–388.

48. Sakai, *Zensho,* pp. 42–54.

49. See ibid., pp. 54–55; and Kuribayashi Norio in *Ajia rekishi daijiten* (Tokyo: Heibonsha, 1959), vol. 2, pp. 416–417.

50. Thus George Chang, in his study of the village elder system, speaks of the *xiangyue* as a system of "village lectures" taken over by the local gentry from the village elders in the mid-Ming period, without noting the original significance of the term, its provenance from Zhu Xi, or how it became attached to village lectures. (*Ming Studies* 7, p. 58.)

51. See Sakai, *Zensho,* pp. 49–54; Lu Shiyi, *Shi zheng lu,* Jiangsu shuju 1892 ed., ch. 5 Xiangjia yue; Joanna F. Handlin, *Action in Late Ming Thought* (Berkeley: University of California Press, 1983), pp. 47–51, 139–140, 199–203; Kandice Hauf, "The Community Compact in Sixteenth Century Jian Prefecture, Jiangsi," *Late Imperial China* 17:2 (December 1996), pp. 1–50.

52. *Wang Yangming quanshu* (Taipei: Zhengzhong shuju 19), vol. 3, pp. 279–282, *Instructions for Practical Living,* trans. Wing-Tsit Chan (New York: Columbia University Press, 1963), p. 299.

53. *Quanshu,* vol. 3, p. 280; Chan, *Instructions for Practical Living,* p. 299: "As long as they have a single thought to do good, they are already good people. Do not be proud that you are good citizens and neglect to cultivate your personal life. As long as you have a single thought to do evil, you are already evil people. Whether people are good or evil depends on a single instant of thought."

54. See Sakai Tadao, "Yi Yulgok and the Community Compact," in de Bary and Haboush, *The Rise of Neo-Confucianism in Korea,* pp. 323–348.

55. Joseph McDermott, "The Community Pact in Ming China," paper presented at the Conference on Ritual and the State, Paris, June 1995, p. 16.

56. Ibid., pp. 9, 14, 16.

57. Ibid., pp. 21–22, 26–30, 40–41.

58. Suzuki Kenichi, "Son-raku no kyōiku" (Local Education in Ming China) in Taga Akigoro, *Kinsei Ajia kyōikushi kenkyū* (Tokyo: Bunri shoin, 1966), pp. 691–718.

6. *Chinese Constitutionalism and Civil Society*

1. *Huang Ming zuxun,* in *Mingzhao kaiguo wenxian,* vol. 3, *1579–1591,* Edward Farmer, trans. (Taipei: Hsüeh sheng shu-chü, 1966), 4 vols.

2. This is the judgment of the leading Western authority on Song law, Brian McKnight, conveyed in a personal communication.

3. See my "Chen Te-hsiu and Statecraft," in Robert P. Hymes and Conrad Schirokauer, *Ordering the World* (Berkeley: University of California Press, 1993), p. 362.

4. Wm. Theodore de Bary, *Waiting for the Dawn: A Plan for the Prince* (New York: Columbia University Press 1993), p. 99. Some portions of what follows here are drawn from this earlier work.

5. Ono Kazuko, "Tōrinha no seiji shisō," *Tōhō gakuhō*, 1980, pp. 266–282, particularly emphasizes the combination of legal restraints on the ruler and the institutionalization of public discussion in academies as an attempt by Donglin scholars to subject dynastic rule in the late Ming to a higher constitutional law.

6. Yamanoi Yū, *Kō Sōgi* (Tokyo: Kōdansha, 1983), pp. 73–76. In discussing the role of the Prime Minister and other reforms to curb the ruler in the MITFL, Yamanoi repeatedly uses the word "check" in transliteration. On this point see also Mizoguchi Yūzō, *Chūgoku zenkindai shisō no bussetsu to tenkai* (Tokyo: Tokyo University Press, 1980), pp. 267–268; and Li Jinquan in Wu Guang, *Huang Zongxi lun* (Hangzhou: Zhejiang guji chubanshe, 1987), p. 328.

7. Luo Huaching, "Gong chi shifei," *Huazhong shiyuan xuebao*, September 1984, pp. 55–58.

8. There is sometimes a tendency to equate the "progressive" thinking of seventeenth-century Enlightenment scholars as if they fell into a uniform emerging pattern, as when Tang Zhen's discussion of the education of the Crown Prince is likened to Huang's proposal for the Court and the Heir Apparent to attend the discussion at the Imperial College. Tang Zhen would subject the Heir Apparent to a rigorous experience of life and work among the peasants, which may have the same value as later Maoist policies for the reeducation of intellectuals in the countryside, but has the opposite effect from establishing an autonomous public space for intellectuals, as Huang would have it. See Xiong Yuezhi, "Huang Zongxi yu Tang Zhen fandui fengjian zhuanzhi zhuyi te sixiang," in *Shanghai shifan daxue xuebao, zhexue shehui kexue*, 1973:3, pp. 27–31.

9. For the less favorable connotation attaching to *jiangxue*, even as it may be used by the same author to mean: "vapid, groundless, pedantic discussion," see Yamanoi, *Min Shin shisōshi no kenkyū* (Tokyo: Tokyo University Press, 1980), p. 271, and my own discussion of Huang's contemporary Lü Liuliang in *Learning for One's Self*, pp. 278–282.

10. On this question in the late Ming see Ono, "Tōrinha no seiji shisō," *Tōhō gakuhō* 28, 1958, pp. 266–267; and Mizoguchi Yūzō, *Zenkindai shisō* (Tokyo: Tokyo University Press, 1980), pp. 14–16.

11. See my *Waiting for the Dawn,* p. 109.

12. Lynn Struve, "The *Changes* in Early Qing Court Classicism," in draft manuscript shared with the author.

13. See my *Waiting for the Dawn,* pp. 71–85.

14. See his *Sibian lu jiyao, Siku quanshu zhenpen* ed., 12:1a–3b; 18:5b–6b, 11ab (vol. 724:100–101, 152–155).

15. This section is based in part on contributions by Peter Zarrow and Joan Judge to chapter 31 of the second edition of Wm. Theodore de Bary et al., eds., *Sources of Chinese Tradition* (New York: Columbia University Press, 1998).

16. Liang Qichao, Xinmin shuo, in *Yinbing shi wenji* (Shanghai: Zhonghua shuju, 1926), 12:40b–47ab.

17. Liang Qichao, *Xinmin shuo* in Taiwan, Zhonghua shuju, 1959. 8:31–32, 38–39, translation and commentary by Peter Zarrow for the second edition of de Bary et al., eds., *Sources of Chinese Tradition.*

18. Ibid., 6:16–18, 22–23.

19. See de Bary and Lufrano, eds., *Sources of Chinese Tradition,* vol. 2, p. 107.

20. The foregoing is based on the work of Joan Judge. See her *Print and Politics: Shibao and the Culture of Reform in late Qing China* (Stanford: Stanford University Press, 1996), esp. part II.

7. Women's Education and Women's Rights

1. "Xinminshuo" in *Yinbing shi wenji* 12:40b–41a.

2. Wm. Theodore de Bary and Richard Lufrano, eds., *Sources of Chinese Tradition* (New York: Columbia University Press, 1998), vol. 2, pp. 153–156.

3. He Zhen, *"Nüzi fuchou lun,"* pp. 7–23; translation adapted from that of Peter Zarrow for de Bary et al., eds., *Sources of Chinese Tradition.*

4. M. Huc, *A Journey Through the Chinese Empire,* 2 vols. (New York: Harper & Bros., n.d. [Author's preface dated 1854]); London edition of 1859, author identified as Evariste Regis Huc, vol. 1, pp. 257–260, 262–264.

5. Ban Gu, *Bohudong delun,* Sibu congkan ed., 7:15a–16a.

6. *Hou Hanshu* 84, Zhonghua ed., p. 2789.

7. *Nü xiaojing, Nüsishu,* xia, 15a–21b (Tokyo: Naikaku bunko ed. 1854), adapted from translation by Theresa Kelleher.

8. *Mingshi* 128:3784–3788; in L. C. Goodrich and C. Y. Fang, eds., *Dictionary of Ming Biography* (New York: Columbia University Press, 1976), pp. 1023–1026, Biography of Chou Tao-chi (Zhou Daochi) and p. 606, Biography of Hsü Ta (Xu Da), by Edward L. Farmer.

9. *Mingshi* 128:3784–3788; *DMB,* pp. 1225–1231, Biography by F. W. Mote.

8. Chinese Communism and Confucian Communitarianism

1. Liu Shaoqi, *How to Be a Good Communist* (New York: New Century, 1952), p. 16.

2. Ibid., p. 17.

3. Ibid., p. 31.

4. Despite Liu's attempt to appropriate and redefine Confucian cultivation for Communist purposes, he and this specific text were later attacked by Mao during the Cultural Revolution for attempting to resurrect "Confucian individualism." See Yan Jiaqi and Gao Gao, *Turbulent Decade: A History of the Cultural Revolution,* trans. Daniel W. Y. Kwok (Honolulu: University of Hawaii Press, 1996), p. 139.

5. See Roderick MacFarquhar, *The Origins of the Cultural Revolution,* vol. III: *The Coming of the Cataclysm* (New York: Oxford University Press, 1977), ch. 18.

6. Adapted from the translations of Catherine Lynch for the second edition of Wm. Theodore de Bary et al., eds., *Sources of Chinese Tradition* (New York: Columbia University Press, 1998), ch. 33. The excerpts are from Liang Shuming, *Theory of Rural Reconstruction (Xiangcun jianshe lilun).* Zouping Xiancun shudian 1937; reprinted in *Liang Shuming quanji,* vol. 2 (Jinan: Shandong renmin chubanshe, 1989). The following account also draws upon Professor Lynch's paper, "The Idea of Community in the Thought of Liang Shuming," presented to the Conference on Confucianism and Human Rights, East-West Center, Honolulu, Hawaii, May 22–24, 1996.

7. *Liang Shuming quanji,* p. 51.

8. Ibid., p. 40.

9. Ibid., p. 145.

10. Ibid., pp. 174–176.

11. Ibid., pp. 199–201.

12. Ibid., pp. 205–206.

13. See Wm. Theodore de Bary, *The Message of the Mind* (New York: Columbia University Press, 1989), pp. 146–151.

14. Lu Shiyi, *Sibianlu jiyao,* Zhengyi tang quanshu ed., 18:11a–13b (Siku quanshu zhenben ed. 724:155–156). See his plan for "Ordering the Community by Three Compacts" *(Zhixiang sanyue)* in *Lu Fouding xiansheng yishu,* 1900 ed. of Tang Shouqi, ce 18, pp. 1a–15a.

15. See Ron Guey Chu, "Chen Te-hsiu's *Classic of Governance:* The Coming of Age of Neo-Confucian Statecraft," University Microfilms, 1988, pp. 68–72, 350–355; and Richard Von Glahn, "Community and Welfare" in Robert P. Hymes and Conrad Schirokauer, eds., *Ordering the State* (Berkeley: University of California Press, 1993), pp. 221–254.

16. *Zhixiang san yue,* in *Lu Fouding Yishu,* ce 18, 2b–4b.

17. See *Liang Shuming quanji* (Jinan, Shandong renmin chubanshe, 1989), vol. 2, pp. 320–345. For further on Liang Shuming's communitarian thought, see Catherine Lynch, *Liang Shuming and the Populist Alternative in China* (Stanford: Stanford University Press, 1998).

18. *The Wall Street Journal,* May 27, 1994, p. A6.

19. From Wm. Theodore de Bary, "China's Prospects in Historical Perspective," in Sol Sanders, ed., *The U.S. Role in the Asian Century* (Lanham, Md.: University Press of America, 1997), pp. 72–75.

20. *The New York Times,* Sunday, March 16, 1997, sec. 13, p. 4.

21. *Zuozhuan,* Duke Xiang 14th, trans. adapted from Burton Watson, *The Tso-chüan* (New York: Columbia University Press, 1989), p. xvi.

22. Quoted more fully in Wm. Theodore de Bary, *The Trouble With Confucianism* (Cambridge, Mass.: Harvard University Press, 1991), pp. 82–83.

23. *Guoyu,* Zhou yu I, trans., adapted from Watson, *The Tso-chuan,* pp. xvii.

Afterword

1. Stanford: Stanford University Press, 1957.

2. Mark Van Doren, *Liberal Education* (New York: Holt, 1943), p. 127.

3. See Wm. Theodore de Bary and Ja-Hyun Kim Haboush, *The Rise of Neo-Confucianism in Korea* (New York: Columbia University Press, 1985).

Works Cited

Andrew, Anita M. "The Local Community in Early Ming Social Legislation: Ming Taizu's Approach to Transformation and Control in the 'Great Warning.'" *Ming Studies* 20, Spring 1985.

Ban Gu, *Bohudong delun*. Sibu congkan ed.

Berry, Thomas. "Individualism and Wholism in Chinese Tradition: The Religious Cultural Context." Paper prepared for the ACLS/NEH-sponsored conference held at the Breckinridge Center, York, Maine, June 24–29, 1981.

Bloom, Irene, J. Paul Martin, and Wayne L. Proudfoot, eds. *Religious Diversity and Human Rights*. New York: Columbia University Press, 1996.

————, trans. "Mencius." In Wm. Theodore de Bary and Irene Bloom, eds., *Sources of Chinese Tradition*. 2nd ed., vol. 1. New York: Columbia University Press, 1998.

Chan, W. T. *Instructions for Practical Living*. New York: Columbia University Press, 1963.

————. *Reflections on Things at Hand*. New York: Columbia University Press, 1967.

Chang, Chung-li. *The Chinese Gentry*. Seattle: University of Washington Press, 1955.

Chang, George Jer-lang. "The Placard of People's Instructions." *Ming Studies* 7, Fall 1978.

Chen Xianzhang, in *Chen Baishaji*. Wenyuange siku quanshu 1246/19–20.

Chow, Kai-wing. *The Rise of Confucian Ritualism in Late Imperial China*. Stanford: Stanford University Press, 1994.

Chu, Ron Guey. "Chen Te-hsiu and the 'Classic on Governance': The Coming of Age of Neo-Confucian Statecraft." University Microfilms, 1988.

————. "Scholarly Autonomy and Political Dissent in Local Academies of the Early Ch'ing." In *Chung-kuo wen-chih yen-chiu chi k'an*. Taipei: Academia Sinica, March 1993, no. 3.

―――. "Rites and Rights in Ming China." Paper presented to the Conference on Confucianism and Human Rights, East-West Center, Honolulu, Hawaii, August 14–17, 1995.

Dardess, John W. *Confucianism and Autocracy*. Berkeley: University of California Press, 1983.

de Bary, Wm. Theodore. *Self and Society in Ming Thought*. New York: Columbia University Press, 1970.

―――. *Neo-Confucian Orthodoxy and the Learning of the Mind-and-Heart*. New York: Columbia University Press, 1981.

―――. *The Liberal Tradition in China*. Hong Kong: Chinese University Press of Hong Kong, 1983.

―――. *The Message of the Mind*. New York: Columbia University Press, 1989.

―――. *Learning for One's Self*. New York: Columbia University Press, 1991.

―――. *The Trouble with Confucianism*. Cambridge, Mass.: Harvard University Press, 1991.

―――. *Waiting for the Dawn: A Plan for the Prince*. New York: Columbia University Press, 1993.

―――. "Chen Te-hsiu and Statecraft." In Robert P. Hymes and Conrad Schirokauer, eds., *Ordering the World*. Berkeley: University of California Press, 1993.

―――. "China's Prospects in Historical Perspective." In Sol Sanders, ed., *The U.S. Role in the Asian Century*. Lanham, Md.: University Press of America, 1997.

―――, ed. *The Unfolding of Neo-Confucianism*. New York: Columbia University Press, 1975.

――― and Ja-Hyun Kim Haboush, eds. *The Rise of Neo-Confucianism in Korea*. New York: Columbia University Press, 1985.

――― and J. Chaffee, eds. *Neo-Confucian Education*. Berkeley: University of California Press, 1989.

――― and Tu Weiming, eds. *Confucianism and Human Rights*. New York: Columbia University Press, 1997.

――― and Irene Bloom, eds. *Sources of Chinese Tradition*, vol. I. 2nd ed. New York: Columbia University Press, 1998.

――― and Richard Lufrano, eds. *Sources of Chinese Tradition*, vol. II. 2nd ed. New York: Columbia University Press, 1960, 1998.

Elman, Benjamin A. *Classicism, Politics and Kinship.* Berkeley: University of California Press, 1990.

——— and Alexander Woodside, eds. *Education and Society in Late Imperial China, 1600–1900.* Berkeley: University of California Press, 1994.

Farmer, Edward L. "Social Order in Early Ming China." In Brian McKnight, ed., *Law and the State in Traditional East Asia.* Honolulu: University of Hawaii Press, 1987.

———. "Social Legislation of the First Ming Emperor: Orthodoxy as a Foundation of Authority." In Kwang-ching Liu, ed., *Orthodoxy in Late Imperial China.* Berkeley: University of California Press, 1990.

French, Howard. "Africa Looks East for a New Model." *New York Times,* February 4, 1996, 4:1.

Goodrich, L. C. and C. Y. Fang, eds. *Dictionary of Ming Biography.* New York: Columbia University Press, 1976.

Han shu, Zhonghua ed. Beijing: 1971.

Handlin, Joanna F. *Action in Late Ming Thought.* Berkeley: University of California Press, 1983.

Hauf, Kandice. "The Community Compact in Sixteenth-Century Jian Prefecture, Jiangsi." *Late Imperial China* 17:2 (December) 1996.

He Zhen. *"Nüzi fuchou lun."* Trans. Peter Zarrow. In Wm. Theodore de Bary and Richard Lufrano, eds., *Sources of Chinese Tradition.* 2nd ed., vol. 2. New York: Columbia University Press, 1998.

Ho Ping-ti. *The Ladder of Success in Imperial China.* New York: Columbia University Press, 1962.

Hou Hanshu. Beijing: Zhong hua ed., 1974.

Hsün tzu: Basic Writings. Burton Watson, trans. New York: Columbia University Press, 1962.

Huang Ming zhishu. Taipei: Cheng-wen, 1969.

Huang Ming zuxun. In *Mingzhao kaiguo wenxian,* vol. 3, 1579–1591. Taipei: Xuesheng shuju, 1966, 4 vols.

Huazhong shiyuan xuebao, September 1984.

Huc, M. *A Journey through the Chinese Empire.* 2 vols. New York: Harper & Bros., n.d. [author's preface dated 1854]; London edition of 1859, author identified as Evariste Regis Huc.

Hymes, Robert P. and Conrad Schirokauer, eds. *Ordering the World.* Berkeley: University of California Press, 1993.

Johnson, David, Andrew Nathan, and Evelyn Rawski. *Popular Culture in Late Imperial China.* Berkeley: University of California Press, 1985.

Judge, Joan. *Print and Politics: Shibao and the Culture of Reform in Late Qing
    China*. Stanford: Stanford Univresity Press, 1996.

————. Translation and commentary in Wm. Theodore de Bary and
    Richard Lufrano, eds., *Sources of Chinese Tradition*. 2nd ed., vol. 2.
    New York: Columbia University Press, 1998.

Keenan, Barry. "Diary Pedagogy in Lower Yangtze Academies
    1830–1900," Yuelu Academy conference, "Confucianism and Edu-
    cation," Changsha, China, August 1996.

Kelleher, M. Theresa, trans. *Nü xiaojing, Nüsishu, xia*. Tokyo: Naikaku
    bunko ed. 1854. Also in Wm. Theodore de Bary and Irene Bloom,
    eds., *Sources of Chinese Tradition*, vol. I. 2nd ed. New York, Columbia
    University Press, 1998.

Kimura Eiichi. "'Sitte' to Shushi no gaku." In *Chūgoku tetsugaku no
    tankyū*. Tokyo: Sōbunsha, 1981.

Kuribayashi Norio. In *Ajia rekishi daijiten*. Tokyo: Heibonsha, 1959.

Landauer, Frederic and Huang Chun-chieh, eds. *Imperial Rulership and
    Cultural Change in Imperial China*. Seattle: University of Washington
    Press, 1994.

Late Imperial China. Pasadena, Calif.: Society for Qing Studies, vol. 17.

Lee, Thomas H. C. "Academies: Official Sponsorship and Suppression."
    In Frederic Landauer and Huang Chun-chieh, *Imperial Rulership and
    Cultural Change in Imperial China*. Seattle: University of Washington
    Press, 1994.

Leung, Angela. "Elementary Education in the Lower Yangtze Region
    in the Seventeenth and Eighteenth Centuries." In Benjamin A.
    Elman and Alexander Woodside, eds., *Education and Society in Late
    Imperial China, 1600–1900*. Berkeley: University of California Press,
    1994.

Li chi. James Legge, trans. New Hyde Park, N.Y.: University Books, rpt.
    1967.

Li Laizhang. *Li Shanyuan quanji*, Kangxi 43 (1704) ed.

Li Mengyang. *Kongtongji*, Siku quanshu zhenben.

Liang Qichao. *Yinbing shi wenji*. Shanghai: Zhonghua shuju, 1926.

————. *Xinmin shuo*. Taiwan: Zhonghua shuju, 1959.

Liang Shuming. *Theory of Rural Reconstruction (Xiangcun jianshe lilun)*.
    Zouping Xiancun shudian 1927, or Liang Shuming quanji vol. 2.
    Jinan: Shandong renmin chubanshe, 1989.

Littrup, Leif. *Subbureaucratic Government in Ming Times*. Oslo: Univer-
    sitetsforlaget, 1981.

Liu, Kwang-ching, ed. *Orthodoxy in Late Imperial China.* Berkeley: University of California Press, 1990.

Liu Shaoqi. *How to Be a Good Communist.* New York: New Century, 1952.

Lü Liuliang. *Sishu jiangyi.* 1686 ed.

———. *Sishu yülu.* Tiankailou, 1684 ed.

Lu Shiyi. *Lu Fouding xiansheng yishu.* 1900 ed. of Tang Shouqi, ce 18.

———. *Shi zheng lu.* Jiangsu shuju, 1982 ed.

———. *Sibian lu jiyao, Siku quanshu zhenben* ed., vol. 724.

Luo Huaching. "Gong chi shifei," *Huazhong shiyuan xuebao,* September 1984.

Lynch, Catherine. "The Idea of Community in the Thought of Liang Shuming." Conference on Confucianism and Human Rights, Honolulu, Hawaii, East-West Center, May 1996.

———. *Liang Shuming and the Populist Alternative in China.* Stanford: Stanford University Press, forthcoming.

MacFarquhar, Roderick. *The Origins of the Cultural Revolution,* vol. 3. New York: Oxford University Press, 1997.

Mair, Victor. "Language and Ideology in the Written Popularizations of the Sacred Edict." In David Johnson, Andrew J. Nathan, and Evelyn S. Rawski, *Popular Culture in Late Imperial Culture.* Berkeley: University of California Press, 1985.

McDermott, Joseph. "The Community Pact in Ming China." Conference on Ritual and the State, Ecole Francaise d'Extreme Orient, Paris, 1995.

McKnight, Brian. *Law and the State in Traditional East Asia.* Honolulu: University of Hawaii Press, 1987.

Miao xue dianli. Siku quanshu zhenben, ed. Chengzong shili xiaoxue shushu.

Ming Taizu. *Jiaomin bangwen.* In *Huang Ming zhishu,* vol. 3. Taipei: Zhengwen, 1969.

Mingshi. Zhong hua, ed. Beijing, 1974.

Mingzhao kaiguo wenxian. Vol. 3, 1579–1591. Taipei: Hsüeh sheng shuchü, 1966, 4 vols.

Mizoguchi Yūzō. *Chūgoku zenkindai shisō no bussetsu to tenkai.* Tokyo: Tokyo University Press, 1980.

———. *Zenkindai shisō.* Tokyo: Tokyo University Press, 1990.

The New Republic. July 14, 1997.

The New York Times. March 16, 1997, sec. 13.

Nüsishu. Tokyo: Naikaku bunko ed. of 1854.

Ono Kazuko. "Tōrinha no seiji shisō." *Tōhō gakuhō* 28, 1958.

Polachek, James. "Literati Groups and Group Politics in Nineteenth-Century China." Ph.D. diss., University of California, 1977.

Rawski, Evelyn. "Economic and Social Foundations." In David Johnson, Andrew Nathan, and Evelyn Rawski, eds., *Popular Culture in Late Imperial China.* Berkeley: University of California Press, 1986.

Rowe, William T. "Education and Empire in Southwest China." In Benjamin A. Elman and Alexander Woodside, eds., *Education and Society in Late Imperial China, 1600–1900.* Berkeley: University of California Press, 1986.

Sakai Tadao. *Chūgoku zensho no kenkyū.* Tokyo: Kobundō, 1960.

———. "Yi Yulgok and the Community Compact." In Wm. Theodore de Bary and Ja-Hyun Kim Haboush, eds., *The Rise of Neo-Confucianism in Korea.* New York: Columbia University Press, 1985.

Sanders, Sol, ed. *The U.S. Role in the Asian Century.* Lanham, Md.: University Press of America, 1997.

Sen, Amartya. "Asian Values and Human Rights." Hans Morgenthau Memorial Lecture, Carnegie Council on Ethics and International Affairs, New York, May 1, 1997. Published in *The New Republic,* July 14, 1997, pp. 33–40.

Shanghai shifan daxue xuebao, zhexue shehui kexue, 1973:3.

Shizuwen. Zhu zi daquan, Sibu beiyao ed.

Song Lian, *Song xueshi wenji,* Sibu congkan ed.

Struve, Lynn. "The *Changes* in Early Qing Court Classicism." Draft manuscript.

Su Tianjue. *Guochao wenlei.* Sibu congkan ed. Also in Wenyuange Siku quanshu ed., vol. 1367.

Suzuki Kenichi. "Son-raku no kyōiku" (Local Education in Ming China). In Taga Akigoro, *Kinsei Ajia kyōikushi kenkyū.* Tokyo: Bunri shoin, 1996.

Taga Akigoro. *Kinsei Ajia kyōikushi kenkyū.* Tokyo: Bunri shoin, 1966.

Ubelhör, Monika. *Neo-Confucian Education.* In Wm. Theodore de Bary and J. Chaffee, eds., *Neo-Confucian Education.* Berkeley: University of California Press, 1989.

Van Doren, Mark. *Liberal Education.* New York: Holt, 1943.

Van Glahn, Richard. "Community and Welfare." In Robert Hymes and Conrad Schirokauer, eds., *Ordering the World.* Berkeley: University of California Press, 1993.

The Wall Street Journal. May 27, 1994.

Wanyong zhengzong. In *Riyong leishu,* preserved in the Hōsa Bunko, Nagoya.

Wang Yangming. In *Wang Wencheng gong quanshu,* Wen yuange Siku quanshu ed.

Watson, Burton, trans. *Hsün tzu: Basic Writings.* New York: Columbia University Press, 1962.

————, trans. *The Tso-Chüan.* New York: Columbia University Press, 1989.

Wu Guang. *Huang Zongzi lun.* Hangzhou: Zhejiang guji chubanshe, 1987.

Xiong Yuezhi. "Huang Zongxi yu Tang Zhen fandui fengjian zhuan-zhi zhuyi te sixiang." *Shanghai shifan daxue xuebao, zhexue shehui kexue,* 1973:3.

Xu Heng. "Shiwu wushi." In *Luzhai quanshu* in Chūbun, Kindai kanseki sōkan ed., 2nd series, vol. 5. Kyoto, 1975.

Xu wenxian tongkao. Shanghai: Commercial Press, Shi tong ed.

Yamanoi Yū. Min Shin shisōshi no kenkyū. Tokyo: Tokyo University Press, 1980.

————. *Kō Sōgi.* Tokyo: Kōdansha, 1983.

Yan Jiaqi and Gao Gao. *Turbulent Decade: A History of the Cultural Revolution.* Trans. D. W. Y. Kwok. Honolulu: University of Hawaii Press, 1996.

Yu, Anthony C. "Altered Education." Remarks delivered at the fortieth anniversary of Hong Kong Baptist University, April 1996. Published in *Criterion* 35:2, Spring/Summer 1996, Divinity School of the University of Chicago.

Yuan wen lei. Siku quanshu zhenben ed.

Yu Ji. "Jingshi dadian xulu." In Su Tianjue, *Guochao wenlei,* Sibu congkan ed.

Yu Ji. "Shucheng xian ming-lun-tang ji." In *Yuan wen lei,* Siku quanshu zhenben ed.

Zarrow, Peter, trans. Liang Qichao. *Xinmin shuo.* In Taiwan, Zhonghua shuju, 1959. Translation and commentary for Wm. Theodore de Bary and Richard Lufrano, eds., *Sources of Chinese Tradition,* vol. II. 2nd ed. New York: Columbia University Press, 1998.

Zhang Boxing. *Zhengyi tang quanshu,* Siku quanshu zhenben ed.

Zhixiang sanyue. In *Lu Fouding xiansheng yishu,* 1900 ed. of Tang Qi, ce 18.

Zhu Xi. *Zhu zi daquan,* Sibu beiyao ed.

————. *Daxue zhang zhu.* Taipei: Zhongguo zixue minju jicheng ed. 1978.

————. *Meng zi ji zhu.*

Zuozhuan. Duke Xiang 14th. In Burton Watson, trans., *The Tso-Chüan.* New York: Columbia University Press, 1989.

Index